T0291216

Blueprint for Engagement

Authentic Leadership

Blueprint for Engagement

Authentic Leadership

Norma T. Hollis, MS, BCC

Contributions by

Betty Kimbrough, BS

Former Vice President of Human Resources at Target Stores

Peggy Muhammad, BSN, RN

Dr. Dexter S. Russell, DN

A PRODUCTIVITY PRESS BOOK

Routledge
Taylor & Francis Group
711 Third Avenue, New York, NY 10017

Productivity Press is an imprint of Taylor & Francis Group, an Informa business

Printed on acid-free paper

International Standard Book Number-13: 978-1-138-74713-5 (Hardback)
International Standard Book Number-13: 978-1-315-18029-8 (eBook)

Library of Congress Cataloging-in-Publication Data

Names: Hollis, Norma T., author.
Title: Blueprint for engagement : authentic leadership / Norma T. Hollis.
Description: New York : Taylor & Francis, [2018] | Includes bibliographical references and index. |
Identifiers: LCCN 2018002617 (print) | LCCN 2018010000 (ebook) | ISBN 9781315180298 (eBook) | ISBN 9781138747135 (hardback : alk. paper)
Subjects: LCSH: Leadership. | Communication in management. | Teams in the workplace.
Classification: LCC HD57.7 (ebook) | LCC HD57.7 .H635 2018 (print) | DDC 658.4/092--dc23
LC record available at https://lccn.loc.gov/2018002617

Visit the Taylor & Francis Web site at
http://www.taylorandfrancis.com

and the CRC Press Web site at
http://www.crcpress.com

This book is dedicated to the people who have
helped make authenticity come alive.

Tracey Carruthers, my friend and mentor for longer than we both
realize. Your ability to help me 'see' what I could not has been priceless.
My focus on authentic leadership could not have been sustained
nor this book written without you. I have eternal gratitude.

Linda Walker, my right and left hands. Without you, I could not have stayed
on path to gain the knowledge that translated into this book. Your unwavering
support and assistance have helped me keep my sanity through some very
difficult and uncertain times. I could not have done it without you.

To all the Authentic Voice Protégés and Authenticity Ambassadors who helped
me realize the quality and breadth of the Authenticity Grid. Without your
participation and encouragement, this book would not have been possible.

And finally, to the thousands of people who follow me on social media, on
my newsletter list, have heard me speak live, on radio or internet, thank
you for your constant encouragement and validation of my work.

May all of us benefit from engagement and authenticity,
to be better people, to lead a better world.

Contents

Foreword

The world we live in is chaotic at best, and this chaos translates into industry and healthcare and affects the success of organizations all over the globe. The leadership competencies of the past do not provide the skill to transform organizations in this current environment. Modern leadership competencies focused on leveraging the staff by engaging them and recognizing them as key to unbridled success are what is necessary during these times. The key to engaging the staff is found in one simple word, *trust*. Trust is the most difficult thing to earn but the easiest to lose. Once a leader has lost the trust of their staff, the climb back to that status is far more difficult. An important factor in the acquisition of trust is the notion of authenticity. The authentic leader is "real" to their employees and creates an environment of calm and inclusivity that makes the employees feel valuable, which translates into increased engagement.

Norma Hollis in her book, *Blueprint for Engagement: Authentic Leadership*, takes the reader on a journey to developing their authentic self that will translate into behaviors and success in the workplace. Norma has developed her own unique approach to the concept of authenticity and shares her knowledge, theories, and concepts with the reader. She takes you through what she describes as her three voices of authentic leaders, which include the inner voice, the outer voice, and the expressive voice, all of which need to be in balance to form the platform for authenticity and self-awareness. This is truly a unique approach and interesting read.

I met Norma several years ago at a workshop and have been a fan of hers since. I find her to be authentic in every aspect of her life as well as willing to teach and mentor others in these concepts. I have also had the opportunity to attend one of her workshops to actually experience the process to improving my own authenticity. I now teach this skill to all of my leaders as vital to their success and growth.

When I explore publications to read that I feel will enhance my own development as a leader, I look to the expertise and background of the author. Norma Hollis has been on the pioneering edge of this concept of authenticity. She demonstrates incredible knowledge in this area as well as experience in the effective translation of the concept to others.

I feel honored to write this foreword for her latest book because I truly believe in the value of this important skill. As an educator and leadership expert myself,

I can attest to the value and depth of knowledge you will receive. So, whether you are a seasoned executive or emerging leader, *Blueprint for Engagement: Authentic Leadership* will provide you with one of the most important modern competencies for effective leadership. Don't miss this valuable opportunity to learn from Norma.

Val Gokenbach DM, RN, MBA, RWJF
Senior executive, Baylor Scott and White Health
Owner, Dr. Val, Leading Leaders
National Speakers Association (NSA) speaker
Leadership expert and author

Author

Norma T. Hollis is a human development specialist who is an international authority on authenticity and self-awareness. She is a Board Certified Coach who has consulted at Fortune 500 companies; directed large non-profits; coached C-suite executives; and written programs for authentic leadership, building dynamic teams, and creating engaging corporate cultures.

Hollis spent 30 years researching human nature from multiple perspectives to determine what makes people and organizations "authentic." The result is her Authenticity Grid and Authenticity Assessment, tools she developed and uses to help people gain self-awareness, self-acceptance, and self-management. Her programs address key attributes of authentic leadership and offer frameworks that inspire engagement in the workplace.

Her background includes a BS degree in child and family sciences and a MA degree earned from life experience. In her first career she spent over a decade directing and writing developmental programs for child care facilities. In her second career, Hollis was the first African-American woman to own a speakers bureau for ethnic speakers. Now she consults, trains, coaches, and licenses organizations and individuals to develop authentic leaders, empower engaging teams, and increase capacity for effective communication.

She is the author of *Ten Steps to Authenticity* and *The Process to Become a Professional Speaker* and has created numerous workbooks, audios, and video programs. She was identified by Wellness Council of America as one of the Top 100 Professionals in the Health Promotions Industry in 2014 and was selected as one of 16 individuals to represent the United States on a five-week visit to China in 2018 where she taught an expanded version of the Authentic Voice System to university students through the World Academy for the Future of Women.

Chapter 1

Why We Need Authentic Leaders

Authentic leaders are a special breed of people. They know who they are, and this self-knowledge empowers them to transform their life and the lives of those they lead. Their authenticity builds loyalty, trust, collaboration, engagement and commitment. It forges positive change in their teams, their company, their community and their industry. They are the new, emerging force in our ever-changing evolution as human beings.

Authentic leaders evolve as humans evolve, and they forge the innovative evolution of business. Leadership that suited us a century ago does not work well now. Likewise, what works well now will not be the norm a century from now, perhaps, even 20 years from now. This makes the role of authentic leaders increasingly important because they are the leaders who are at the front of change.

The need for authentic leaders has accelerated in recent years. One reason is because some leaders in the corporate world still view leadership from the style that was developed in the Industrial Age. Our world moved to rapid manufacturing techniques starting in 1760. That's when it became clear that production could be increased with an assembly-line process where employees performed a single or simplified task as quickly as possible. The goal was to lead employees to work faster, more efficiently and to produce higher numbers of product in shorter timeframes.

Leadership focused on the ability to motivate faster performance. There was little concern with the personality of the employee, what they brought to the table as an individual and how much personal satisfaction they gained from the job. If employees were not happy, management just replaced them with other 'robot-like' workers who could do the job faster.

Today's world is different. We are experiencing the Digital Age, where employees are expected to think critically on multiple topics using all the readily available information to build on current knowledge. Leadership in this era motivates employees to perform their best by identifying problems, offering solutions, taking action and communicating soundly.

As we continue to evolve we can peek at the coming focus, which is the Empowerment Age. This period encourages companies to recognize employees' natural, authentic gifts and talents and integrate those attributes into the work environment. This view of the role of the employee is in stark contrast to the Industrial Age orientation. Companies that are able to make the transition are the ones that will last over the long run. Those who miss this evolutionary curve will cease to meet the needs of employees and their effectiveness will likely dwindle.

The two questions all leaders must ask themselves are; first, to what degree they are still modeling Industrial Age thinking and management styles, and second, how to transform themselves and their organizations to leave Industrial Age thinking and evolve through the Digital Age to an Empowerment Age style of leadership.

The answer lies in *authentic leadership.*

Authentic leadership is transformational leadership. It transforms people from Industrial Age styles of thinking and behaving to a culture of empowerment and engagement. It emphasizes ethics, honesty, sincerity, integrity and relationship-building through honest communication between leaders and team members. While Industrial Age leadership emphasized profit and share price over people and ethics, authentic leadership achieves the same profit and share price objectives, but the process is different. Authentic leadership creates positive environments and enthusiastic teams. Performance is generally higher because team members have mutual respect and recognize the value that each member brings – they enjoy coming to work.

Authentic leadership is accomplished by authentic leaders who know themselves and lead with an awareness of their shortcomings and how to compensate for them. This awareness of self allows them to build rapport, improves the quality of their communication skills, and their ability to engage their workforce. They are role models for their organizations, and society as a whole.

Authentic leaders have attained self-awareness, self-acceptance and self-management. Not only do they know who they are, they have accepted themselves with full awareness of their strengths and vulnerabilities. They have learned how to manage themselves with effective ways to fill their gaps. They know that a vulnerability is not a weakness; it's just someone else's gift. They know they are not perfect and do not have expectations of perfection from themselves or from team members. Instead, they equip their team with members who collectively fill gaps not only from the technical side of business but also from the 'soft skills' side so that harmony exists within the team. The experience of coming to work then becomes something to look forward to.

Leadership is an experience. It is an action word. To experience leadership is to go through the actions of leading or being led. Leaders experience leadership differently than those who are being led.

The experience for the leader is the act of personally observing, encountering and undergoing something. No matter how many people are led or what they are being led toward or away from, leaders *will* go through a personal experience, encountering challenges and undergoing successes. It is a unique type of learning.

The experience for those being led is the act of being transformed, the process of going through change, the first-hand experience, transformation.

Authentic leadership leads people through change and, in the process, empowers them to new levels of communication and performance. It's a win for the leader, the employee and the organization. They are role models for their organizations and society as a whole.

That is the transformational experience of authentic leadership.

In *Blueprint for Engagement* you will learn traits of authentic leaders and how leaders use these traits to empower their teams. The blueprint provides a foundation for leaders seeking to approach their role with greater authenticity.

Why a Blueprint Is Needed

A lot of what we do in life is through what I call 'self-navigation.' We decide what we want and go after it. We may take classes, go to seminars or read books to help us learn what to do. Sometimes we just jump in. We use the knowledge gained and lessons learned from experience to seek success in our endeavors. Unless we have a mentor or coach we are generally self-navigating our way through each day.

Many factors determine whether we achieve what we are seeking. Sometimes we do not get the benefit of school or training or are not able to apply what we have learned to our goal. In these cases, we generally rely heavily on our self-navigation skills. Or maybe we cannot find the type of training that we need. This path generally takes a lot longer because without a coach, a manual or a blueprint, it's hard to know what to do or how to predict the consequences of our decisions. A blueprint provides the steps needed.

This is especially true of authenticity. Although the word has been around for a long time, it is not universally understood. The current conversation began around 2007, especially during the presidential campaign, when we all asked: Is Hillary Clinton authentic? Is Barack Obama authentic? The word was also frequently used on television shows like *American Idol* when contestants were deemed 'so authentic.'

During this time, we lacked an understanding of what authenticity meant, although there were a lot of scholars talking about it. Harvard Business Review Press published *Authenticity: What Consumers Really Want* by professors James Gilmore and B. Joseph Pine II. Many other authors began to emerge who discussed authenticity and the need for authentic leadership. There was universal agreement on one significant point: *The first step to attaining authentic leadership is self-awareness.* This *Blueprint for Engagement* provides the important next step: 'how' to gain the self-awareness that leads to authentic leadership.

Self-awareness is only the beginning step. Once self-awareness is achieved, the next step is self-acceptance. Many people strive for perfection and seek to turn their weaknesses into strengths. The authenticity approach refers to weaknesses as vulnerabilities. We are vulnerable in areas of life where we are not very skilled or gifted. We can choose to spend our energy strengthening a vulnerability or we can find people on our team who have strengths where we do not. Authentic leaders accept their vulnerabilities and find ways to fill their gaps.

This knowledge helps the authentic leader with self-management, an important aspect of being authentic. Authentic leaders manage themselves and their teams so that they lead from strengths. When teams have authentic respect for others' strengths and vulnerabilities and share a vested interest in the success of the team, goals are generally achieved. Authentic leaders accomplish this success.

Anyone can embark on a journey to self-navigate their way to authentic leadership. The path is clearer and more effective with a blueprint, a map, a step-by-step guide, a system, that provides the ability to 'see' self, accept vulnerabilities and make small 'tweaks' that promote self-management.

Chapter 2

The Three Voices of Authentic Leaders

After studying human nature for over three decades from personal, professional and spiritual perspectives, I learned what it means to live with authenticity.

It started when I was 28 years old and had done everything my parents said to do. I had the husband, nice cars, a house on a hill, good jobs – all the things they said would make me happy, and I was miserable. I didn't like what I was doing nor who I was with. My mother seemed to think that if I had a degree in education and a teaching certificate I would always be able to get a job. The only thing she didn't consider was that I didn't like teaching in a classroom. I only lasted 30 days then had to find another way to make a living.

Likewise, with the husband. By all outer appearances he was a great catch, but to me he was far too aggressive and his goal of becoming a multimillionaire took over much of his thinking. I was very happy in non-profit organizations making a difference in the world and it was hard to adjust to his values, which drove him to business practices that I felt uncomfortable with.

That's when I started the quest to understand myself. I didn't feel I could decide what to do with my life unless I figured out who I was. I had no idea the journey would take me down a 30-year path. Along the way I directed large non-profits, was the first black woman to open a speakers' bureau for black speakers and discovered and developed the Authenticity Grid, which is the foundation of *Blueprint for Engagement*. I also went through a lot of experiences that strengthened my authenticity and helped me to heal from childhood trauma related to debilitating earaches and being a highly creative child in a house of highly traditional family members. Some of these experiences, and their lessons, will be shared later in this book.

What I learned about myself in the first part of this 30-year journey was that I had a lot of different energies flowing through my body. I began to focus on these energies and experience their characteristics.

The first thing that I noticed was that I have three characteristics to myself. I began to call these my three voices. Later I learned that others resonated with the idea of three voices too. We each have these three voices. They are our Inner, Outer and Expressive Voices.

Inner Voice
The Inner Voice is the voice that speaks from within. This is a silent and private superconscious voice that whispers in many ways. This Inner Voice thinks, communicates and moves you to action.

Outer Voice
The Outer Voice represents other people's perceptions. It is brand, first impression, reputation, presence, charisma. It is what others see and how they interpret behavior and appearance.

Expressive Voice
This Expressive Voice represents 'who' a person has become and how one's life is lived. It's whether or not natural gifts and talents are shared with the world, daily habits and personality.

In summary:

Inner Voice	Outer Voice	Expressive Voice
Speaks from within	Perception of others	Self-expression

When I gained this initial understanding, I felt that it wasn't enough. It helped me 'see' parts of myself but didn't explain the multiple energies I felt within. I needed to know more. I explored deeper and found three energies within each of the three voices. Some of these energies were inquisitive and thoughtful, others liked to play with words and still others enjoyed being active. I identified these energies as thinking, communicating and doing, then realized that as humans, we generally spend our life either thinking, communicating or doing. We are engaged in at least one of these at all times.

I reflected on my personal leadership experiences, which started very early in life as valedictorian of my elementary school and an officer in my high school graduating class. My professional leadership has included directing large non-profits and leading several hundred employees and self-navigating the business world as the owner of a speakers' bureau and coaching company.

Reviewing my background, I discovered that I was most successful in leadership roles when I took the time to *Think* about an issue, then *Communicate* it with others before taking action and *Doing* something. There were many times when I worked on committees or started a new job and I was asked to 'do' something before I was given an understanding of what I was to accomplish. And there were times when I told employees to 'do' something without communicating my expectations or giving them time to think about the task. I just wanted them to 'do' something, get a task accomplished.

These understandings became the concepts for energies within that I simply refer to as *Think, Communicate* and *Do*. I use these terms to refer to an effective process for task accomplishment.

Think

This is the first step in the process of accomplishing a task successfully. First, *Think* about the situation. This means gaining a cognitive awareness by doing research, comparing options, giving assessments, seeking information, reading, going on the Internet, studying, training, observing, reflecting – using multiple resources to collect information about the situation encountered.

Communicate

Sharing your information with as many sources as appropriate, feasible and possible. It means talking, asking questions, listening, reading and writing. It might mean writing in a journal or even writing a contract or entering into an agreement. It might mean broad communication through the media or being a guest on a talk show. Whatever the genre, the verb is 'communicate' and it involves sharing knowledge and gaining knowledge. It is the way to test the thoughts acquired during the *Think* stage. Generally, *Communicate* occurs between two or more people. Sometimes *Communicate* can be within, for example, through meditation or prayer.

Do

This is the final stage, which is the action stage. Frequently, people get involved in the action stage before going through the first two steps. When we act before thinking, it is difficult to achieve the goals we have set. When sufficient thinking and appropriate communication take place, the *Do* portion flows effortlessly.

In summary, the *Think – Communicate – Do* process is a three-step process:

1. *Think* – research and evaluate
2. *Communicate* – seek additional perspectives
3. *Do* – take action

Each of these three energies – *Think, Communicate* and *Do* – are within the three voices.

Inner Voice

Think:	*Intuition* – sixth sense – listening to and following Inner Voice
Communicate:	*Integrity* – values – obtaining and following a belief system
Do:	*Inspiration* – drivers – personal internal and external motivation

Outer Voice
Think: *Net Wellness* – general state of health – holistic wellness and balance
Communicate: *Network* – associations – the quality and quantity of relationships
Do: *Net Wealth* – abundance – how signs of wealth are displayed

Expressive Voice
Think: *Legacy* – natural gifts and talents – recognizing and sharing natural gifts and talents with the world
Communicate: *Likeability* – personality – sharing best self
Do: *Lifestyle* – habits – day-to-day activities

This turned into a grid that I refer to as the Authenticity Grid, which is below.

The Authenticity Grid then grew into a comprehensive program, called the Authentic Voice System (AVS), to assist individuals and organizations to understand the value of and gain the tools to live and lead with greater authenticity. The system includes workbooks, videos, audio, interviews, classes, events and a host of other activities and products, a collection of the vast amount of knowledge that I gained after 30 years of research and another six years of applying the information and witnessing the results.

Understanding and applying the principles of the Authentic Voice System provide a vehicle for self-awareness, self-acceptance and self-management. The remaining chapters will provide the blueprint for understanding the Authenticity Grid, the foundation of the AVS and applying its principles to everyday life and leadership.

The Authenticity Grid

	INNER VOICE	OUTER VOICE	EXPRESSIVE VOICE
THINK	**INTUITION** *Listening to and following your Inner Voice* Are you listening and responding to the private voice within yourself?	**NET WELLNESS** *Hollistic wellness and balance* How do your thoughts on various aspects of wellness show up in your life?	**LEGACY** *Recognizing your natural gifts and talents* Are you using your gifts in ways to communicate to the world?
COMMUNICATE	**INTEGRITY** *Obtaining and following a belief system* What does your value system communicate to those who are listening?	**NETWORK** *The quantity and quality of your relationships* What do your associations say about you?	**LIKEABILITY** *Your personality* What does the person you expose to the world say to the world about who you are?
DO	**INSPIRATION** *Personal internal and external drive* What drives you – the Inner Voice of inspiration or the Outer Voice of motivation?	**NET WEALTH** *Abundance* How do you display your signs of wealth?	**LIFESTYLE** *Your day-to-day activities* How do your habits speak to who you are?

Many perceive the nine dimensions of the Authenticity Grid as composed of 'soft skills.' In the Industrial Age, soft skills were not important to the bottom line. In today's world and the world that is facing us, soft skills make the difference between an organization with an engaging culture and one that is struggling to find its place in the new world.

In subsequent chapters of *Blueprint for Engagement* are guidelines, not only for applying the Authenticity Grid to the self, but also to the organization. References will be made to the Corporate Authenticity Grid, which is below. However, the Corporate Authenticity Grid is not the focus of this book. This book's primary purpose is to help you, the individual leader, deepen your awareness of self so that you can lead more effectively, more authentically. This concept is aligned with academic and entrepreneurial literature that states that the number one quality of an authentic leader is self-awareness.

This blueprint provides strategies for raising authenticity to such a level that it will positively impact self-awareness and therefore leadership skills. If you would like to go to the next step and apply the concepts to your organization, you will see contact information at the end of this book.

The Corporate Authenticity Grid™

	EMPLOYEE	ORGANIZATION	COMMUNITY
THINK	**INTUITION** *Listening to and respecting ideas of employees* How does the company value the ideas and suggestions of employees?	**NET WELLNESS** *Holistic wellness and balance* What is the wellness of the company's triple bottom line? (economic, ecological, social)	**LEGACY** *Recognizing natural gifts and talents* How is the company using the gifts and talents of employees? How are the company's gifts and talents shared with the community?
COMMUNICATE	**INTEGRITY** *Obtaining and following a value system* What does the company value? How do these values show up in the company's mission statement and interaction with employees' community?	**NETWORK** *The quantity and quality of relationships* What are the company's strategic alliances? Who does the company do business with?	**LIKEABILITY** *Brand, marketing and PR* How is the company liked/perceived in the marketplace?
DO	**INSPIRATION** *Internal and external drive* How does the company inspire its employees?	**NET WEALTH** *Abundance* What does the company do with its profits? How are profits tied to employees and community?	**LIFESTYLE** *Day-to-day activities* Are company habits consistent with values? How do values and habits show up?

Understanding the nine energies that are in the grids (referred to as dimensions) and integration of them into day-to-day life will enable the development of an organizational culture that empowers employees on all levels. These employees become inspired to engage with the company, produce at peak performance, contribute to the evolution of the business and generally feel great about themselves and their contribution.

Being authentic is the answer to transformational leadership. It starts with transformation of self, which leads directly to transformation of the organization. The more a leader knows about self, the more the leader can understand others. When a leader walks in authenticity, the result becomes leadership where there are no regrets.

The following pages will help you understand yourself as you understand the Authenticity Grid. At the end of each chapter you will find a question that is taken from the Authenticity Assessment. Answer the question and write your score on the grid in Chapter 6. When you complete this book, you will receive further instructions to attain and interpret your score.

The Authenticity Grid is the blueprint. The chapters that follow will give guidance on how to use the blueprint and emerge as an authentic leader.

Although space is given within this book to reflect on many of the exercises, you will gain even more value from this book if you start a journal to record your thoughts. You can purchase a spiral notebook, start a video, audio or text file on your computer or phone, or any other way you may have to record your thoughts. There are so many options. Select the one that best fits your lifestyle and be ready to take notes when it is suggested or when you feel a desire to reflect. Recording your thoughts as you go through the process of engaging with this book will give you lots of information about yourself and be valuable in your growth process.

Chapter 3

Inner Voice Blueprint

Life emanates from the inside. Would there be life without an Inner Voice? Is life just what people can see from outer appearances, or is life based on the thoughts that go on in the mind?

I ask these questions to point out the importance of the Inner Voice. Life starts from the inside. Our day begins, not just when we open our eyes from a night's sleep, but when we say to ourselves, "Wake up." We are moved to action by the thoughts that go on inside. This is part of our Inner Voice and it is the foundation for day-to-day living.

The Inner Voice is a private voice only heard by its owner. It has been called a personal GPS system, connecting us with intangible aspects of life that as a society we know exist; however, don't fully understand.

Everyone has an Inner Voice. Some people get acquainted with their Inner Voice early in life, some never recognize its existence. But it's there. The Inner Voice provides internal dialogue, sometimes a monologue. It's 'you' talking to 'you.' Years ago, talking to oneself was considered to be 'crazy.' Now it is widely accepted that we all talk to ourselves.

Every day we have a verbal stream of consciousness that flows within us. It's there when we ask ourselves what we will wear or what we will eat. It's there when we berate ourselves for something we said or did – or didn't say or do. And it's there when we congratulate ourselves for success.

Even though we all have this internal speech, because it takes place so naturally, effortlessly and quietly, we often miss its message. It is sometimes the fleeting idea that darts so quickly between our conscious thoughts that it is missed. It may be the internal conversation that takes place in our head. It is not an outside source that speaks to us from the outside. We can't see the bearer of the words we receive. And generally, we don't 'hear' loud voices; it's more like sensing thoughts, a knowingness or maybe seeing images. It's listening at a deep level.

When I recognized this voice within me I was going through a very difficult time in my life. I was eight years old and had just come out of the hospital, where a culture was done on a discharge from an infection that came from a hole in my eardrum. The culture and hospital visit were not difficult. What was difficult was what happened after the hospital. I was discharged after a one-day stay to test different ways to put a halt to the infection. They only found one thing that would work. I went to my doctor's office the next day. It was an ear-nose-throat doctor who sat me in his dentist-like chair. Once I got settled the nurse stood at my feet and my mother at my left side.

The doctor told me he could stop the infection but that it would hurt. I was a pretty resilient eight-year-old, full of energy, and had no qualms about what was going to happen next, although the positioning of my mother and the nurse should have given me a clue.

The doctor pulled out an instrument that looked like a very long sewing needle. He put cotton on the end of it then dipped it into a clear liquid. He then put a metal cone in my right ear as he turned my head to the side, then slowly inserted the instrument into my ear canal as he held my head tightly.

The next thing I felt was a pain that was as if acid was eating the inside of my ear. I hollered and hollered and hollered. It took some time for me to calm down and when I left the doctor's office I had to keep my head tilted to the side because each time I moved my head the liquid would find another place to cause pain.

I walked ever so slowly out of the doctor's office and as my mom drove home I kept telling her to slow down because each turn of the wheel seemed to move the liquid to a new area. It was quite a painful experience, which shaped my life in many ways.

The adults in my life were sympathetic to my pain; however, they really didn't know how to deal with it. My family was not very good at communication and even worse at helping me deal with my emotions. And they didn't put me in therapy, so I was left to fend for myself to deal with the pain and seek normalcy in the process.

I also had to go back to the doctor's office to have the treatment done again and again. This was followed by another year of very intense earaches that could not be stopped even though I was given shots, ear drops and pills. It was a very challenging time in my life.

When the adults didn't talk to me about what I was going through, my Inner Voice kicked in. It would talk to me, soothe me, direct me and generally guide me in many areas of my life and has done so my entire life.

But at the young ages of eight and nine, and without the benefit of family communication, I was left to decipher this voice on my own. When my Inner Voice first started speaking to me I ignored it, but it was persistent. I finally gained the courage to talk back to my Inner Voice. I told that voice that I wasn't sure if it was real – maybe I was just hearing voices. I told the voice that if it was a real voice I should listen to, prove it to me. I asked the voice to give me evidence by showing me someone in the next week who was wearing red socks. I also asked that someone mention the word 'elephant' in a conversation within the next week.

I then began to pay close attention to every person who crossed my path and to listen deeply to each conversation I was engaged in to see if someone walked by with red socks or the word 'elephant' was mentioned. In less than a week both of the requests were fulfilled. A student walked in front of me wearing red socks and a friend mentioned the word 'elephant' in a conversation.

I was blown away and absolutely delighted, although a little scared. One success was not enough for me to totally believe this voice, so I made similar requests over the next five weeks and each time, I was given evidence that my Inner Voice is real.

As a result, I have developed a very intimate relationship with my Inner Voice. I recognize it to be somehow connected to what I call 'unseen supporters' that are all around but that we are unable to see.

People refer to their Inner Voice in many ways – inner guide, spiritual guide, ancestors, holy spirit, unconscious mind, angels – there are many ways to identify it. Having an Inner Voice is a normal part of being human. It's important to recognize it and learn to trust it.

When I took my inside journey to understanding myself at age 28, I began by dissecting my Inner Voice. By that time, my voice and I had a 20-year relationship, so I was pretty comfortable understanding how it worked within me. I learned that my Inner Voice has three parts to it. I call the parts 'dimensions' because they are dimensions of our consciousness and work together internally.

The three dimensions are Intuition, Integrity and Inspiration. These are three important dimensions of authentic leaders. In fact, it is within the Inner Voice that authenticity begins. The Inner Voice is one's connection to the unseen parts of life that we still do not understand but many of us accept. We know something exists even though we do not know why or how; we just learn to accept it over time.

Authentic leaders are connected to their Inner Voice. They use their Inner Voice as a sounding board and as a source for information and direction.

The Intuition, Integrity, and Inspiration sections will give a deeper understanding of Inner Voice and its dimensions. Since authenticity begins in the Inner Voice, authentic leadership also begins within the Inner Voice. Leaders who are authentic listen to and trust their Inner Voice.

A. Intuition – Authentic Leaders Master Their Intuition

What Is Intuition?

Inner Voice and Intuition are often used synonymously. While they are very similar, the two are not the same. Intuition is a part of Inner Voice. It refers to the act or faculty of knowing or sensing without the use of rational processes, the ability to listen to the voice that speaks within. Even more, it is the act of responding to the voice within. It is not ego. Intuition is connected to feelings; it is generally a 'felt' experience where Inner Voice is the combination of heart and head, feeling and intellect.

Intuition is the voice of the soul and the language of the heart. It is the unseen messenger that delivers important messages to guide each person's life.

The intuitive voice a very subtle voice that whispers quietly and can be hard to access in the midst of the noise of daily life. Seldom does it yell. It is found in the space between words thought and spoken. Hearing one's Intuition generally happens when the mind is quiet. It sometimes takes practice to make the connection and 'hear' accurately. It's like listening to the language of the heart and the gut.

The intuitive voice is the voice of the universe. It's is the voice of the invisible parts of self that seem to have knowledge beyond the reality of this world. It is a sixth sense.

The intuitive voice exists to assist and direct and comes from a place deep within that seems to know what is best. Learning to recognize this voice, listen to it and then respond to it enables alignment with it. This results in developing a relationship, a partnership with this voice, and entering into an ongoing conversation that leads to greater good. Finding the intuitive voice, learning to listen to it, then trusting it and responding to it appropriately can lead to a rich and fulfilling life. It is a basic foundation for authentic leadership.

Some people refer to Intuition as a hunch – having a feeling that something is going to happen, someone should be called or an action should be taken. It's an advance knowledge that sometimes makes no sense because it is generally not specific, it comes from the subconscious part of self.

Intuition is a *Think* energy because we are born with the ability to be intuitive. However, even though we are born with the gift, most of us have to learn how to use it accurately. Many of us even have to learn that the voice even exists.

Authentic leadership begins with having a solid connection with personal Intuition and applying it appropriately to self and team members.

How Do Authentic Leaders Find Their Intuition?

The first step to increasing ability to connect intuitively is to recognize Intuition.

Learning to 'listen' at this subconscious level and practicing on a regular basis will increase skills.

When my voice started speaking to me at age eight, I spoke back. From that point on I have been in constant conversation with my intuitive voice. I don't always get the messages right and sometimes I am thoroughly confused. But I never stop the communication and do my very best to listen, interpret and respond. Here is the six-step blueprint to help you recognize, respond to, develop and apply your intuitive skills to your organization.

Step #1: Recognize That You Talk to Yourself

Whether you realize it or not, you talk to yourself, probably every day. You have an Inner Voice that responds to the questions you ask it each day. Pay attention when you hear yourself quietly ask, "What am I going to wear today?" or "What time is it?" or "What shall I have for dinner tonight?" or any of the many questions you ask yourself daily. Catch yourself when you ask yourself, then stop and listen for the answer. See how you answer yourself, how the answer comes and how quickly.

Some of the ways people answer themselves are with a thought, an image, a memory, a feeling, a smell, a warm rush, or it could be something totally different. How does your voice get your attention?

When you ask yourself what to eat, does a picture come to your mind of something you enjoy eating, does your stomach churn with a craving for a specific food, does your mouth water, do you see yourself in front of the stove or at a particular restaurant? How does your intuitive voice give you the message?

What about when you are deciding what to wear? What process do you go through? Do you match your mood with a certain color? Do you smile while thinking about how a particular outfit led to great compliments or how it made you feel?

Notice whether you struggle for an answer and think about it for a while or whether it comes right to you. Observe yourself in the process of listening to yourself and answering the everyday questions you ask.

Spend several days, weeks or months with this – however long it takes for you to recognize the voice that answers you when you ask everyday questions.

Step #2: 'See' Your Thoughts

Find a time and place where you can be private and quiet for 30 minutes or so. Perhaps you have a favorite chair or a favorite place outdoors. Maybe your home is so busy, the only place you can find solitude is in the bathroom or the closet. Wherever the best place is for you, find it and plan to spend 30 minutes of uninterrupted time there.

When you have found that time and place, go to it and sit quietly. Feel free to set a mood for yourself with candles and other fresh fragrances. Please, no music just yet. Your objective here is to listen to yourself and that is difficult to do when you have music competing for your attention, even if it is just in the background.

Sit comfortably and close your eyes. Sitting with your feet flat on the floor is a good way to get grounded and balanced. Close your eyes and allow your mind to be still. Forget about the work day, your family, what you are going to eat, the many things you have to do – forget about all of that. Just sit quietly, breathe comfortably and allow your mind to be free. Let it wander where it wants to go. Smile so you are promoting a pleasant attitude.

Be still for a while before you read further. Just sit quietly in this space and listen to yourself breathe. If you fall asleep, that's OK.

****

It is difficult to sit still without thinking. Note that you are thinking most of the time. Pay attention to what you are thinking about. See the words or pictures going through your mind. Don't grab any of them, just let them wander through your mind at will. Recognize that these pictures of people and things, the words you are seeing, hearing and feeling – these are your thoughts – this is you talking to yourself. Reflect on the thoughts you had while you were quiet.

Step #3: 'Hear' Your Thoughts

We each engage in self-talk – talking to our self about our self. This conversation is often done at a very deep and unconscious level. Do you know whether you tell yourself you are great or whether you put yourself down? Many of us put ourselves down. We may do so unconsciously and be totally unaware. We might be really passionate about self-improvement, doing and being more. Yet we find we cannot progress, and we don't know why. One reason may be due to negative self-talk.

Self-talk, like Intuition, is a voice that speaks from the unconscious self. This voice is the one that praises or berates its owner. It's the voice that says, "good job" or "you could have done better." It is influenced by the past, has deep effect and in many ways is the foundation for self-esteem.

When your self-talk becomes more positive, your intuitive ability rises as well as your ability to interpret intuitive messages.

In this exercise, you will 'hear' your self-talk by examining and exploring the thoughts you unconsciously have about yourself. I learned this technique from Tony Robbins in his book *Awaken the Giant Within*. The exercise is designed to get you to realize how you are communicating with yourself on an unconscious level.

In Step #2 you learned how to listen to yourself thinking. Now that you know that you think, and you can access your thinking, you will go a little deeper and access what you are thinking on a subconscious level.

This exercise is best done on a day when you will have the ability to be actively engaged in something and still be able to take notes. When I did this exercise, it was a day when I was conducting a training session. I would speak for about 90 minutes, then my partner would speak. In between each of my speaking assignments I was able to make notes about what I was thinking.

That is exactly what you are going to do – take notes about what you are thinking. Each phrase you can hear and remember yourself saying to yourself, you are going to write down. You will learn most if you do this consistently for several hours, a full day or even several days so that you can uncover what you are saying to yourself about yourself.

I was amazed when I reviewed my comments. In a half-day I had a full page of comments such as, "I sure didn't do that right," "I should have…" and "I wish I had…." There were no comments on my sheet that praised or congratulated me for a job well done. I was putting myself down in each comment. No wonder I wasn't feeling all that great about myself. No wonder my self-esteem was not as high as it could have been. No wonder I wasn't happy. No wonder I was having so much trouble leading my team. I was probably thinking about team members in similar ways and my thoughts about myself probably didn't make me a great role model. Just reading the statements I was saying to myself about myself was a real eye-opener. I have since dramatically changed my self-talk. I'm happier, more positive, more successful and a better leader.

Now it's your turn. Listen to yourself talk to yourself. In the morning, what do you say to yourself when you wake up? When you have eaten breakfast, what do you say to yourself? When you are driving to work, what do you say to yourself about your driving? What did you say about what you chose to eat? Begin to write these down. Take an activity you do – perhaps a sport, a game you play, a competition you enter, something that puts you in front of others – something that puts you in a position to elevate or denigrate yourself – and see what your thoughts are. Listen to the words you say to yourself as you are doing the exercise. Listen to what you say to yourself when you have accomplished or failed to accomplish your task. These words are your self-talk. Write them down.

Step #4: Analyze Your List

Take a look at the list of statements you have made to yourself. Examine whether they are mostly positive or negative. What does this say about you? How do you think this affects your leadership style? Would you like to be led by a leader who thinks about self the way you do?

How can you reword your negative statements so that they are positive? Rewriting the statements and making a conscious effort to think positive thoughts is an important factor in becoming an authentic leader.

Step #5: Analyze Yourself

The reason for turning your negative self-talk into positive is to clear your mind to be more receptive and accurate about messages from your intuitive voice. If your self-talk is negative you are more likely to reject intuitive voice messages.

Think about how you feel when you answer the question about what to eat, what to wear or what time it is. Think about times when you feel good about the answer you get. Maybe it's one of your favorite foods or you get it from a favorite restaurant or really enjoy preparing it. Perhaps it's an article of clothing that makes you look and feel great, perhaps your treat to yourself after you lost weight. Or maybe when you look at the clock and it's time to start a date with an important person, or time to go home from work or for your favorite TV show to start. Think about the joy you feel in all of these situations.

This is the feeling you are looking for and striving to feel every day, all the time. It is also how you can feel when your voice speaks to you. This is in contrast to how you feel when your self-talk puts you down.

This is also how you want your employees to feel.

This starts with you being a role model. And you are a better role model when you have positive thoughts. Make a conscious effort to think positively about yourself and those around you, team members, co-workers, family and friends. Examine how they respond to your positivity both at work and at home.

Step #6: Apply the Concepts

These concepts help leaders understand the power of Intuition and its value. The deeper value is applying the concepts to leading on a day-to-day basis.

The most effective leaders have empathy and concern for the people they work with and they show it. Not only are they attuned to their Inner Voice, they also recognize that the company has an Inner Voice and it is the employees. Just like it is important for leaders to listen to their own intuitive voice, it is also important that leaders listen to their employees. Authentic leaders listen to and respect the ideas of employees and provide opportunities for employees to share their ideas and suggestions. Authentic leaders give consideration to these ideas and suggestions and seek to implement those that add value to the company.

Think – Communicate – Do

Life is about action and once you have listened and responded, it means nothing unless you act. When you asked yourself what you were going to wear, then you gave yourself an answer, the next step was to actually get the clothes and put them on. Without this activity, the exercise was futile. The action had to be done to complete the process – you could not walk around without clothes. Likewise, when you asked yourself what you wanted to eat. Obviously, you took action because you found food and are still surviving through eating food. Action is a critical part of the process. To act or not to act – that is the question. It is easy to act on the questions you ask yourself. If you don't answer and act on these questions some of your basic needs might not be met.

Acting on the self-talk question is a little more complex. You are probably currently reacting subconsciously to the talk you give yourself. What you say to yourself and how you react to it could be the basis of some of your self-esteem. If you say you are a positive person and feel good about yourself, yet you find your self-talk is negative and denigrating, then there is an imbalance that needs to be tweaked.

To summarize:

- ***Think*** – listening to your intuitive voice and the voice of your employees
- ***Communicate*** – honest sharing of information within yourself and with team members
- ***Do*** – taking action

Case Study *– Paul is an insurance agent who has been struggling with income for several years. He became a broker so that he could represent multiple companies and build a team to create residual income. It was a struggle. Paul then became more aligned with his Inner Voice. He learned how to 'listen' more carefully and made sure that the voice he was listening to was indeed his intuitive voice. Once he became sure, he received an intuitive message to connect with a new company that had been approaching him. By listening to and trusting his Intuition, he was led to align with the new company and this generated a new product line, new customers and enabled him to catapult his insurance business in record time. He's now a firm proponent of men's Intuition!*

Authenticity Assessment

At the end of each dimension you will be asked a question that is a part of the Authenticity Assessment. When you complete this book, you will have the opportunity to determine and interpret your score. This process will help you to identify the areas of your authentic leadership where your effectiveness can be improved.

When you answer each Authenticity Assessment question, answer it from the perspective of how you have integrated the concept in your life. To understand what I mean by integrate, compare it to when you first learned how to drive a car. Remember, you had to think about how to hold your hand, buckle your seatbelt, figure out how to get where you were going and a host of other thoughts. Now you often wonder how you got home so quickly. The process of driving has been integrated into your day-to-day habits. You rarely have to think about it because it is part of your life, you just do it, it is integrated into your life.

When you answer the questions of the Authenticity Assessment, if the question is something that you have not given any thought to then your response is toward '1.' If it is something that you have considered deeply and have made changes in your life so that the concept is fully integrated, then your response is toward '10.'

Authenticity Assessment Intuition Question

INTUITION is defined as the degree to which you listen to and follow your 'Inner Voice.'

Question: Are you listening and responding to the quiet voice within you?
Response:

A. Score yourself 1 – 3 if you "didn't know you had a voice within"
B. Score yourself 4 – 7 if you "found your voice and are beginning to access it"
C. Score yourself 8 – 10 if you "allow your Inner Voice to lead and direct you"

Circle your response:

1 2 3 4 5 6 7 8 9 10

Transfer the number you circled to Box #1 of the Your Authenticity Assessment Scores grid in Chapter 6.

Authentic leaders are connected to their Inner Voice.

B. Integrity – Authentic Leaders Live with Integrity

What Is Integrity?

Integrity means acting on ideas that are within your value system and discarding those that are not. It is steadfast adherence to moral and ethical principles, soundness of moral character, honesty, personal value system and how the values are lived. Integrity does not expect perfect adherence but does expect consistency and adherence in far greater proportion than not.

Integrity is the step after Intuition. When Intuition speaks, Integrity evaluates whether the intuitive thought is within the value system and should be acted upon or whether the thought should be discarded. Even when we know we should not act on certain ideas and thoughts, we sometimes do so anyway. Other motivators may cause us to act on values that we do not truly believe in. This is human. Integrity exists when you follow your value system not just some of the time, but a high percentage of the time.

Authentic leaders have values that include keeping their word, speaking the truth, doing what they say they are going to do, operating with fairness and maintaining loyalty to the company and its team. Shared values of Integrity breed open communication and mutual respect. A culture of Integrity invites engagement among the workforce.

In a work environment, Integrity is an important foundation to an empowering culture and a valuable quality for authentic leaders. Teams generally align themselves with the values of their leader. When leaders lead with Integrity they are likely to get Integrity in return.

Integrity is on the *Communicate* row of the Authenticity Grid. Integrity is communicated by what is said and done, how often values are adhered to, how you represent and role model the values you believe in. Since I owned a speakers' bureau, I have met many speakers over the years who have impressive, positive messages, using platform skills that would excite any audience. Yet a closer look at their lives reveals they do not live the life they speak of. Some talk the talk but do not walk the walk. They know the values they want to live but they are not living them.

How Do Authentic Leaders Find Their Integrity?

Integrity exists when you know your values and you live them. Recognizing values is the first step to establishing Integrity. We start out in life following the values of our parents. In time, we learn to accept some of our parent's values and reject others. By the time we have lived a few years as adults, we have had the opportunity to meet many other people whose values differ from ours. This causes us to question the values we were born into and begins the process of our gaining clarity on what we truly believe. In time, we develop our own value system. Sometimes we are clear on our values and sometimes we can only identify them if we take time to examine ourselves and our behaviors to determine what is most important to us.

What we believe in, what we appreciate, talk about, think about, what's important to us, how we judge self and others – these are the foundation of our values. When leaders are clear on their values, and when their values are aligned with the company they work with, they are able to create high-Integrity teams that promote the values of the company.

Improved quality of life is one benefit of living with high Integrity. The ability to awaken each morning and live life from a place of being true to values creates a level of comfort that promotes quality of life. This is a very important concept for authentic leaders to grasp. One of the challenges in the workforce is that so many employees are not engaged. I've read research that varies from 70–81% of the working population is not engaged at work. They go to work for the paycheck but are not engaged in the activities they are doing or the people they are working with.

This is something that can be remedied by creating an environment where employees are aligned with the work that is being done and the people they are working with. It helps when employees' values are assessed prior to hiring. Making sure that new employees come to the job with a high adherence to the values of the company is important. This way there is a greater likelihood that the employee will work in Integrity because their values are aligned.

Employees become shadows of their leader. The values that the leader displays will be mirrored by the employees and in time will impact the culture of the team and potentially the company.

Here are the steps to gain clarity on your values and be a role model in your organization.

Step #1: Identify Your Values

Think about the areas of your life that are most important to you from two perspectives. First, think about what comes to your mind and heart when you ask yourself what is important to you. Perhaps it's family, a relationship, church, a hobby, a pet, or it could be your job. Be honest with yourself. Your head may be saying family, but your heart may be saying something else. Be real with yourself. What's important is that your answer is authentic. From this perspective, prioritize up to five things that are most important to you.

The second way to look at what is important to you is from the perspective of how you spend your time. Think about a block of time – a day, a week, a month, a year – whatever period of time you work within. Now think about how you spend this time. How often are you with family, on the job, traveling, vacationing, watching TV, eating – whatever you do, how much time do you spend doing it? Now prioritize the top five. From this perspective, your value is gauged by the amount of time spent. At the top of your list is the activity you that takes most of your time.

When you compare the two lists, what do you learn? For example, is family at the top of list #1 yet near the bottom of list #2? This does not represent alignment. What does this tell you about how authentically you are living your life? How you do one thing is how you do all things. Create a similar comparison using your values at work and see how aligned they are.

Step #2: Identify Your Company's Values

Your company probably has a vision and mission statement. Get a copy of each and circle the words that indicate the company values.

Step #3: Compare Lists

Are your values and those of the company you work for the same? Are there threads of similarities? Where do you find the similarities? How do you feel about this? Are the values different? A little bit or a lot? How do you feel about this?

What is important is that the values are 'aligned.' This means they support each other, they are in alliance, share similar energy and enable you to address both at the same time. When your values and those of the company are aligned, you are best able to be a role model for your team.

Step #4: Examine Personal Values

Let's go a little deeper on personal values. As you gain clarity on your values and those you want to model, you add engagement to both your home and work life. Here are some values statements for you to consider. The intent is to get you thinking about what is important to you, to your workplace and to your family. As an authentic leader, which of these values do you want to possess? Which are important to your family life? Which to your work environment? How can you impact each? These values could be the foundation of rich conversation both at work and at home.

Score these statements with the number that indicates the level to which the statement speaks to your behavior or belief: 5 = always, 4 = most of the time, 3 = sometimes, 2 = seldom, 1 = never.

	5	4	3	2	1
I am honest, truthful.					
People can count on me.					
I constantly try to improve myself.					
I respect other people's points of view.					
I am constantly learning and evolving.					
I am open to different ways of thinking.					
When people upset me, I let them know.					
I value truth.					
I respect the point of view of others.					
I nurture myself.					
I walk away from unhealthy relationships.					
I let go of judging others.					
I look for the good in others.					
I am responsible.					
I am gentle with all people.					
TOTAL POINTS					

Look at your total points per column and create your own assessment of your responses. These are just a few statements for you to consider regarding your personal values. As you read over this list you probably thought of other values you hold that are not mentioned here. While there are no right or wrong answers to this exercise there are some lessons you will learn about yourself and your own values. Reflect on them and how they apply to your work and home lives.

List additional values not mentioned in the previous grid that are important to you:

___

___

___

___

___

___

___

___

Step #5: Integrity

You now have the elements to know your values. Integrity is the degree that you follow your values. It's time to ask yourself about your level of Integrity with both your personal and company values. Are they aligned, and do you have a commitment to each of them? Is the commitment the same? What can you modify? Are you living with Integrity? What can you do about it?

Think – Communicate – Do

Taking time to *Think* about your values will benefit you in the long run. Think about your own values and those of the people you live and work with, the neighborhood you live in, your city, state, country, and planet. Where do you see compatibilities? Where do you see conflict?

Communicate your values to others so you can learn from them and they can learn from you. You may find yourself modifying your values once you have been exposed to the values of others.

Case Study – *Eddie is a chef. He worked for years at a retirement home preparing food for senior citizens. He enjoyed the work and the people he worked for, but not his boss nor his pay. What really got him upset was when someone was hired from the outside to do a job that he was already doing. In his heart, he wanted to speak and touch people's lives. But with bills to pay and an ailing father, he didn't have the money or the courage to make a change. He got involved with the nine dimensions of authenticity and gained the courage to walk out on his job. He announced it to us on one of our Tuesday calls. Everyone on the call burst out in applause because we had been coaching Eddie toward the courage to leave for some time. It was an adjustment for him. But when he recognized that he would not be living his life with Integrity if he continued to work as a chef when he could be making a difference in the lives of so many people, he found a* *way to earn a living, using his gift of gab and his deep sensitivity. He is now enjoying life in ways he had only dreamed of before.*

Authenticity Assessment Integrity Question

INTEGRITY is defined as obtaining and following a belief system.

Question: What does your value system communicate to those who are watching and listening?

Response:

A. Score yourself 1 – 3 if your answer is "I am not aware of my values"
B. Score yourself 4 – 7 if your answer is "I am aware of my values and recognize where I need to strengthen them"
C. Score yourself 8 – 10 if your answer is "My values are fully integrated in my life"

Circle your response:

1 2 3 4 5 6 7 8 9 10

Transfer the number you circled to Box #2 of the Your Authenticity Assessment Scores grid in Chapter 6.

Authentic leaders role-model Integrity.

C. Inspiration – Authentic Leaders Inspire Others

What Is Inspiration?

Inspiration is the internal drive to action. It is stimulation of the mind and emotions to a high level of feeling or activity. Inspiration often causes a sudden creative act or idea. It is often divinely guided or influenced. The root word of Inspiration is 'spirit.' Inspiration refers to being 'in spirit.'

Inspiration is different than motivation. We hear a lot about motivating employees. I suggest our goal is to inspire our teams. Generally, when people are motivated they are responding to the influence of someone or something outside of themselves. Someone else drives them to take an action. The drive is grounded in the feeling that the motivator gave the employee, so the employee is responding to a feeling that was received from an external source.

True transformation comes when the individual is inspired from within. This happens when a lesson is learned, an experience takes place, a sensitivity is lifted, a pain is healed or some other experience where the feeling element is linked to a rise in consciousness. It's understanding something from a new perspective, being touched, being transformed.

How Do Authentic Leaders Maximize Inspiration?

Authentic leaders are inspired to succeed. They do not wait for someone else to motivate them; they have a deep sense of what they are to do, and they do it. This internal Inspiration is critical for success. It is not good enough to have Intuition unless you are inspired to use it in a positive way. Inspiration is the expression of the intuitive voice. It's Intuition in action.

Authentic leaders need to be inspired and they need to inspire their teams.

Authentic leaders inspire themselves by being aware of the things that drive them. These are the thoughts, words, activities and intentions that create excitement and purpose. They are the reasons to get up in the morning, to overcome challenges, to do what needs to be done. It's the feeling that comes from deep within and shouts to be heard. When this Inspiration is related to the work that you do, you are generally very satisfied with your work environment.

One way that authentic leaders touch their team members is when they celebrate them. Something as easy as acknowledging a team member's natural gifts and talents, celebrating the work they have done or just saying "thank you" can make a big difference between an acceptable and an outstanding employee.

Another way is to engage with team members through conversation that builds rapport while showing that you care. People get inspired when they know that you care.

The authentic leader inspires others and is inspired by others. What inspires you? Does your drive come from within yourself or from external sources? Are you more often inspired or motivated? Are you internally or externally driven?

The blueprint for enhancing your Inspiration follows.

Step #1: Determine Whether You Are Driven More by Internal or External Sources

Think about yourself for a minute. What moves you to action? What do you get passionate about and feel that you must follow through with? Do you see yourself as more inspired or motivated?

The lists that follow will help you determine whether you are more naturally inspired or motivated. As you read this list, place a check mark next to the statements that are most representative of you.

People who are internally driven generally:

- Like to be alone
- Keep a diary or journal

- Are independent and strong-willed
- Like to work with or help people
- Like solitary games and activities
- Are sensitive
- Are shy
- Do not draw attention to self
- Are reflective and meditative
- Are quiet
- Would prefer a more rural than urban environment
- Seem to think deeply
- Get advice from books or the Internet
- Have a close circle of friends

People who are externally driven generally:

- Want friends around
- Prefer team sports to those requiring individual effort
- Are friendly
- Don't like to be alone
- Move easily between groups
- Like teamwork
- Like crowds
- Are leaders
- Often think differently than others
- Get along well with others
- Have several close friends
- Like to be involved in social organizations
- Get advice from other people
- Have a wide network of friends

Do you have more traits of those who are more internally or externally driven?

People who are internally driven are not necessarily inspired. However, some traits of being internally driven are necessary to be inspired.

Step #2: Examine Your Drivers

Take time to examine what drives you. Understanding your drive and whether it is internally or externally triggered will assist you in taking the right action more frequently. You will gain greater confidence about your ability to accomplish tasks and you will be more successful.

You need a mix of inspiration and motivation to be successful. When inspiration/motivation and introvert/extrovert are balanced, a powerful person emerges.

Knowing what drives you and understanding as much as possible about your personal process is a strong force. This brings out your passion and raises your quality of life. To help you understand the degree to which you are inspired and/or motivated, consider the source of your drive by examining a few activities.

Step #3: Identify What Drives You to Action

For two or three activities you do in the next week, you are going to determine whether the activities originated because of a thought, from something someone else said, from something you listened to or read, from your gut, Intuition or from some other source. You will also look at whether you gain personal gratification from internal or external sources. Finally, you will look at the degree of balance you have between internal and external drivers. As you find two or three activities to assess, consider at least one major action (starting a new business, changing residence, a new relationship – if none are coming up, consider one from the past) and at least one minor action (went to a party last night, tried a new route to work, a new hairstyle). For each activity that you are assessing, ask yourself the following questions:

- The action – what was the action that took place?
- The experience – what was the experience that moved you to action?
- What moved you – your thoughts, someone else's comment, your feelings, something you read, something you watched?
- Were you moved by internal or external sources?
- What was your level of passion? Were you highly moved and exceedingly passionate, just going through the motions, or something in between?
- Were you satisfied with the result of the experience?

Step #4: Review

Consider how you answered the questions. Are there are any themes that jump out at you? If so, write them below. Perhaps your theme is that your drive comes repeatedly from certain places or circumstances. Or the theme might be words that are spoken, people you are around, places you visit or colors that you see. How did you express or recognize the theme? Was it from your thoughts, something you read or heard or from a person? Search for your themes and write them in your journal. Go to a quiet place and 'listen' for the answers that come to you.

Are most of your drives inspired or motivated?

Number Inspired __________ Number Motivated ___________

Are you balanced in the number of inspired and motivated? Do you want to be?

____

____

____

Think about the type of work you do. Are you happy with it? Does it inspire you? Does it require you to be inspired or motivated? Do you have the appropriate balance?

Think about your family. Do they motivate or inspire you? Is it balanced?

Examine your passion. What is the theme? What gives you the most passion? What inspires you most?

Step #5: Reflect on Your Responses

Can you identify a theme that drives you? When you find the theme that is the foundation of your Inspiration, you have a clearer understanding of who you are and the circumstances you need to surround yourself with to be inspired. It's an interesting understanding of yourself. As you reflect, you may also get some clues to your purpose.

Think – Communicate – Do

Can you *Think* your way to greater Inspiration? Yes, you can. You can increase your Inspiration by expanding your intuitive and introspective skills.

You can also use communication principles to gain greater Inspiration. Communicating more effectively with yourself leads to increased Inspiration.

Listening to your Intuition and living with Integrity will lead you to create a more inspired life. When your actions are inspired, you are positioned for authentically living a life of high quality.

Case Study – *Tracey was over 100 pounds overweight. When she was first introduced to the nine dimensions of authenticity she asked herself why she was obese. Her answer was that she was raped when she was two years old and again when she was 12. She went inside of herself and found solace in food. She ate so much for so long that she stopped looking at herself and held on to the motivation to keep eating to ease the pain. When she admitted her obesity and decided that she no longer wanted to be that size she made a decision. Her decision was her Inspiration to make a 'tweak' in her life. She started to weigh her food, carrying a scale with her everywhere she went. Within eleven months she had released over 100 pounds, had a public makeover and spoke in Paris just a few months later. No one on the outside could motivate her to release her weight. It wasn't until she was internally inspired that she took the steps that put her on her authentic path and changed her life.*

Authenticity Assessment Inspiration Question

INSPIRATION is defined as personal internal and external drive.

Question: What drives you – the Inner Voice of Inspiration or the Outer Voice of motivation?

Response:

A. Score yourself 1 – 3 if your answer is "I need other people to get me motivated"

B. Score yourself 4 – 7 if your answer is "I am equally motivated and inspired"

C. Score yourself 8 – 10 if your answer is "I inspire myself and accomplish my goals"

Circle your response:

1 2 3 4 5 6 7 8 9 10

Transfer the number you circled to Box #3 of the Your Authenticity Assessment Scores grid in Chapter 6.

Authentic leaders inspire their teams.

D. Inner Voice Summary

Authenticity begins in the Inner Voice. Being truly authentic means having a relationship with your Inner Voice and engaging in ongoing communication. The Inner Voice speaks in ways that help us understand and protect ourselves as we evolve. And when we recognize that the Inner Voice of the organization is the employees, we are positioned to be powerful authentic leaders who make a difference in our company and community.

It's helpful to understand how the Inner Voice works. Ideas come through Intuition, then are filtered through Integrity. Each idea that comes to us is quickly evaluated to conform or not with our value system. If it conforms, then we may be inspired to act on it. If it does not conform, the idea is often discarded.

When our connection with our Inner Voice is strong, the process takes place effortlessly. When we are not clear on our Inner Voice relationship, we may not have the inner clarity that leads to effective decisions.

Authentic leaders have taken the time to know and relate to their Inner Voice. They know and trust their voice and allow it to be their inner guide. Likewise, they know and respect their team members and integrate their input into the ongoing leadership of the team. This is a reliable foundation for building engagement in the workplace.

Chapter 4

Outer Voice Blueprint

Everyone has an Outer Voice. It is the voice that speaks to the public about who you are. It is the voice that speaks to the world.

Your Outer Voice is how people see you, how they interpret what you do and how you present yourself. It's the first impression that you make when you walk into a room. People make a judgment about you based on what they see and how they interpret what they see. Their perception has nothing to do with what's going on in your Inner Voice. People cannot know your Inner Voice by just looking at you. The important thing, as it relates to authentic leadership, is that the Inner Voice and Outer Voice give the same message.

I have met many people who just didn't come across as very authentic. In many cases I was unsure why I had a feeling of disconnect with these people. After I understood authenticity, I realized that some people have Inner and Outer Voices that are not aligned, not giving the same message. It's like someone standing in front of a group with a big frown on their face yet saying that they feel great today. The expression on their face clearly paints a picture of someone who is not feeling so great. They become unbelievable.

Authentic leaders have a strong alignment with Inner and Outer Voices. How they look, carry themselves and the people they surround themselves with – all of these speak volumes about the outer self. They are an expression of inner thinking.

When people look at us they see a reflection of how we have taken care of our self – our values about health, wellness, diet, exercise – these are revealed to the person who is looking. That person comes from their perspective and makes an assessment/judgment about us just based on what they see. This is Outer Voice.

The way we dress is also part of our Outer Voice. The choices of clothes speak to values, money and self-esteem. Style selection and color speaks to personality and many people determine our likeability and approachability based on how we dress. This is part of our Outer Voice.

The car we drive, the home we live in, the restaurants we frequent, the jewelry we wear, how we style our hair, the colors of our clothes, the people we associate with – these reveal a perception of us and speak volumes, even when we haven't said a word. Our Outer Voice is an indication of how we live our life.

This section provides the opportunity to look at Outer Voice and how it is lived. There are three dimensions: Net Wellness, Network and Net Wealth.

Net Wellness refers to the sum total of your health – physical, nutritional, dental, mental, the integration of exercise and using natural vs. chemical products in and on your body.

The **Network** section provides a look at the people surrounding you.

The **Net Wealth** section examines the types of abundance you have access to, not just financial wealth, and how you express your abundance.

How you present yourself is a reflection of how you have treated yourself over the years, how you have lived. The things you have focused on are clues to your purpose. The things you have neglected are potentially those that are standing in the way of achieving your purpose. Use this inventory to strengthen your connection with your Outer Voice and strengthen your authentic leadership.

A. Net Wellness – Authentic Leaders Take Care of Their Health

Understanding Net Wellness

Net Wellness is the sum total of your health. It includes not only physical health but also dental, nutritional and mental health, exercise, and the chemical or natural products you put on and in your body. Net wellness represents how you have integrated all aspects of wellness into your life.

Your state of health speaks volumes about you. It is a voice that represents how you have treated and cared for yourself over the years. As your Outer Voice it gives people an immediate impression of what you think about yourself, the energy you carry and, in some degree, your fitness for the job.

Leaders need energy. It takes a lot of mental, physical and emotional energy to lead others. How does a leader maintain the energy necessary to lead effectively and stay healthy?

Our bodies change as we grow. What a person does in their 20s generally has to be modified by the time the person turns 40 and most certainly by their 60s. We have to stay constantly abreast of how our bodies are changing and be willing to make and support needed change. When we do not change, we set ourselves up for health issues that almost always impact our energy and may impede our ability to be the best leader possible. It is difficult to be adequately focused on your leadership role when you are worried about your health.

The solution is to stay abreast of what is going on with your body. One of the things that this means is gaining an understanding of alternative health practices and seeking natural assistance whenever possible. When you receive a medical doctor's diagnosis, why not get a second opinion from a naturopathic or natural health practitioner to see if there are natural ways of regaining your energy?

Well-rounded health is critical for success in life. You live your life in one body and it is up to you to take care of it. How you take care of it is revealed to people when they look at you.

If I had lived my life listening to and following what others said and not going through my *Think – Communicate – Do* process, I would be dead right now. You see, at age eight I developed a perforated eardrum. I woke up one July 5 and found that a brown liquid had oozed from my ear and dried in multiple places on my pillow case. I had a hole in my eardrum, which my father always referred to as a hole in my head. The hole was caused by an infection and the only way it could be treated at that time was through antibiotics.

I then acquired ear infections each and every year of my life until I made some major changes. Each time I had an infection I treated it with antibiotics. Sometimes I took two or three doses per year. Each time I followed the doctor's instructions to take all medications until they were gone – ten days' worth. I did this for 40 years.

Then one year, after several decades of taking antibiotics, I began traveling for business. In January I traveled to Boston and came home to Los Angeles with a sinus infection. The next month I traveled to Texas and came home with an ear infection. In March I traveled again and obtained a kidney infection. In April I went to my medical doctor to see what was wrong with me. I was put through a battery of tests and told that I was in perfect health. In May I could not get out of bed and became quite alarmed.

I went to my *Think* process and began to learn all I could about ear infections and taking antibiotics. I then found a homeopathic doctor who recognized that I was suffering from taking antibiotics so long. While the antibiotics were killing the infections within my body they were also destroying the good bacteria in my system. The good bacteria exists to fight the infection. Without the good intestinal bacteria (called flora), I was creating all kinds of problems within my colon and other parts of my body.

For the previous 20 years I had also been taking antihistamines every day to fight a sinus drip and allergies. I had tried many times to come off the antihistamines but each time I found my sinus drip increased and I was miserable.

One trip to the homeopathic doctor and I was no longer taking antihistamines. I was also treated for the *Candida albicans* I had acquired from taking too many antibiotics. *Candida albicans* is a yeast infection that women sometimes get. Now I had this yeast infection throughout my body – all because I was taking medicine that was supposed to be good for me. Five years after beginning homeopathic treatments I no longer take any medications – chemical or homeopathic. I have lost

30 pounds and gained tremendous energy. My staff could tell you about my ability to out-dance any of them, and I am older than most of them!

Because I took my health into my own hands I am alive today to talk about it. If I had not, I would surely be a statistic by now. Within my family, three of my female relatives have died of digestive cancer. I changed my diet to minimize the possibility of colon cancer, then found myself with a case of multiple kidney stones in both kidneys. When I changed to a low oxalate diet to prevent kidney stones, for the first time since I was eight years old, I didn't have an ear infection! Who would have thought, since I was already eating a healthy anti-cancer diet, that the foods I was eating to avoid cancer would contribute to my kidney stone problem?

I am alive today because I realized that the medical doctors could not help me, and I found a doctor who could. I am alive today because I thought about my situation, researched and evaluated, communicated with others and took action by finding an appropriate doctor and changing some of my habits. I am alive today so that I can share this information with you and encourage you to gain a new level of wellness.

My Net Wellness has greatly improved because by changing doctors I also changed my outlook on life, my eating habits, made changes in my dental health and chose to live my life with a greater emphasis on natural living.

The goal of Net Wellness is to retain energy and gain longevity. I remember giving a seminar on this process to a group of sales leaders a few years ago. At the conclusion, during the Q & A session, several of the sales managers challenged my perspective. They could not make the connection between Net Wellness and selling. Do you see the connection?

Net Wellness is connected to everything. If you are having a health challenge your mind continues to focus on the challenge and this distracts from your work focus. If you are lethargic, negative thinking, without energy you cannot perform at your best. You lose your ability to function at your most authentic level when you are not well. This impacts your sales ability and the role modelling you will represent to your team as their leader.

Here are the steps you can take to create your blueprint for Net Wellness.

Step #1: Evaluate Your Medical Condition

What are your current medical/physical conditions? How do they hold you back from maximum energy? How are you treating them? Are you using chemicals or natural based products? Have you received any assessments from an alternative practitioner? Give this some thought and write some comments in your journal.

Step #2: Examine Your Energy

When is your energy highest?	When is it the lowest?
Time of day ____________	Time of day ____________
Day of week____________	Day of week____________
Time of year____________	Time of year____________
When are you most alert?	When are you drowsy?
Time of day ____________	Time of day ____________
Day of week____________	Day of week____________
Time of year____________	Time of year____________

Are the activities of your work day consistent with the flow of your energy? In other words, if you are more alert in the morning, are you doing activities then that require the most alertness or are you doing activities that require you to be alert at another time of day?

To be as authentic as possible and maximize your energy, arrange your activities around your energy and alertness cycle. If you have to write, lead a meeting or meet with a client, you want to be as alert as possible. Schedule these activities during you high alert times.

Likewise, some activities require more energy than others. Plan these during your high energy times.

Step #3: Body Check

Sometimes leaders are so busy that they don't take time for themselves. Many health issues can be avoided by just taking time to let your body talk to you before it gets to crisis. Authentic leaders stay aware of their wellness needs and address them so they do not become major issues.

If you are not familiar with alternative wellness practices, please allow yourself to be open to the ideas in this section. Participating in the next exercise is an easy way to create a non-threatening alternative practice that may give you new insight.

Part 1: Go to a quiet place. This should be a place where you can be alone for at least 30 minutes without distractions. Find a place to sit and be comfortable.

Think about your physical body. Close your eyes as you breathe deeply. Just sit relaxed and breathing deeply for a few minutes and get comfortable with the silence.

Now, focus on your body from the neck up. See if you can feel the blood running through your veins. Feel the energy that surrounds your body from the neck up. Do you feel any pain? If so, where is it? How is your level of health from your neck up? Do you feel energized and alert or lethargic and drowsy? Send positive energy to your body from the neck up. Visualize your body from the neck up and send feelings of warmth. Picture your blood flowing smoothly and picture yourself gaining greater health as you envision the blood flowing through you. Continue to keep this image in your mind and smile with the image. This is you sending positive energy to yourself.

Now focus on your body from the waist to the neck. Breathe deeply and fill your lungs with air. Feel your lungs. Is there any congestion? Feel your digestive area. Is food clogged there or is it flowing smoothly? Do you feel gas and discomfort or ease? Feel your breast area, men and women. The number of men with breast cancer is accelerating. Feel your breasts and send positive energy to that area. Send positive energy to your body from the waist to the neck. Visualize your healthy lungs that circulate maximum oxygen. Visualize food flowing through your digestive system, leaving important nutrients and allowing unneeded fiber to continue to flow toward your rectum. Visualize your healthy body from the waist to the neck.

Focus on your body from the mid-thigh area to the waist. Focus on the belly button area and visualize waste products flowing through this area and out of your body. Do you feel constipated? Are your stools loose? What does this say about your health? Do you eliminate after each meal? Feel your genital area. Do you feel sexually healthy? Are you respecting your sexual organs and taking proper care of them? Send positive energy to your body from the waist to the mid-thigh area.

Finally focus on your body from the soles of your feet to the mid-thigh area. Do your legs feel strong and able to hold you and move you about as needed? Feel the blood flowing through your limbs. Send positive energy to your body from the mid-thigh area to the bottom of your feet.

Identify the area of your body in most need of positive energy. Focus on that area, visualize health and send positive energy.

Repeat this exercise as often as possible. It will help you move toward a higher level of wellness.

Part 2: Now sit quietly and send positive energy to all parts of your body. Positive energy is sent when you visualize that part of your body and feel the warmth of sunshine flowing through you. Allow your body to bask in the warmth of your energy. Ask your body what it needs from you to be even healthier. Listen to the responses that your body gives you and give them serious consideration.

You send positive energy when you sit quietly and visualize. If there is a part of your body that felt it needed energy when you did the body check, visualize that part of your body and mentally send it positive energy. You can also visualize yourself sending rays of light to that part of your body. This is an alternative practice that can calm you, give you unexpected information about your body and assist you in healing yourself.

Consider, research and/or take action on any symptoms or other potential physical problems you are aware of or became aware of as you completed this exercise.

Step #4: Nutritional Wellness

Your physical wellness will be negatively or positively affected by what you put into your mouth. Health begins with the foods you eat, and this process was initiated when you were a child. The eating habits you have now probably began when you were an infant and unless you made major changes in your diet, you are probably eating the same types of foods that you ate as a child.

A major component of my steps toward health was changing my diet. I was lucky in many respects because my mother raised us on fresh fruits and vegetables. Because I ate them as a child it was easy for me to incorporate them into my diet as an adult. In addition, my immune system was probably strengthened because of my childhood diet. Eating fruits and vegetables is very helpful for healthy development and is particularly important for children.

Before making major changes in my diet I did my normal thinking and communicating. I read books on *Candida albicans* to find out what I should and should not eat. I changed my diet based on what I read, tried new recipes and new foods. It took a little over a year, but I learned which foods would work well for me and which ones would not. I gradually changed my diet to the foods that were nurturing for me.

One of the things that I learned during my research was that we promote health when we eat foods that are 'live.' One way to determine if a particular food is live is to see if it has seeds in it. Food with seeds is live food because when you put the seeds in the ground, they sprout. It is alive, has nutrients to support it and when introduced to additional supportive nutrients, growth takes place. To determine if a food is good for you try this exercise. Plant the food in the ground. If it grows then it will be nurturing for your body. If it does not grow, then it is dead food and will not have as nurturing an effect once you have eaten it. Authentic leaders understand the importance of food. They eat for energy and longevity and are role models for their teams.

It is amazing how many food sources we encounter that sell us food that is not live. You can find fast food restaurants on many corners. I challenge you to put some of the fast food that you eat into the ground to grow. I doubt that it will. Consider what it is doing in your body.

Also, consider eating organic food which is grown without chemicals or pesticides. Did you know that most foods – whether fruits, vegetables or meat – are grown with the aid of chemicals, pesticides, preservatives and often growth hormones? These additives help food grow rapidly and last longer. Organic food does not last as long and is healthier for the body because it is all natural.

Authentic leaders are healthy eaters.

Step #5: Dental Wellness

My father was a dentist. As a result, my teeth were well cared for. A quick look in my mouth a few years ago would have revealed clear evidence of my father's care because I had mercury fillings in most of my teeth. Mercury fillings are obvious to the sight because they are shiny silver. My mouth was full of them.

It wasn't until I began to recover from *Candida albicans* that I learned that the mercury in my mouth was a problem. It was contributing to my low energy and also contributing to the ongoing survival of the *Candida albicans* within my system.

I learned this through reading and communicating with the homeopathic community. You see, mercury is a toxic substance. Mercury fillings have been linked to Alzheimer's disease, gastrointestinal problems, neurological problems and brain damage in children. Research has shown that children can suffer from immune system damage as well. When you have mercury in your mouth, each time you chew food you are releasing the toxins into your system. The toxins stay there for a long time and embed themselves in your organs and can create health problems if not removed properly.

As a result, I had all the mercury removed from my mouth. It was done quadrant by quadrant. What I found interesting was that after the removal of each quadrant, my energy soared. It took about two months to complete the process and at its end I was a new woman.

To remove the mercury the dentist had to completely cover my mouth so that only the area she was working on was exposed. Then she put me on oxygen so that I would not breathe any fumes from the mercury. It seems that the mercury is so toxic that precautions must be made to assure patients don't breathe the fumes.

After the removal I had to go through chelation therapy. This is the process of removing the mercury from my organs. I have since been through a second chelation process because the mercury was so dominant within my system. Chelation is done in several ways; one is to ingest a substance that will remove the metal toxin from your system. After going through this process, I noticed improvement in energy also.

The fillings were replaced with white resin types, such as porcelain. They are not as durable as the mercury; however, they are much healthier.

I had also been suffering with a case of gingivitis. This is the preliminary stage of the major gum problem known as periodontal disease. By paying closer attention to my teeth, flossing nightly, increasing my intake of fruits and vegetables and reducing my intake of sweets, I reversed the gingivitis. Even though my father was a dentist I had no idea that there were so many things to consider that relate to teeth, including your smile.

Smiling is contagious. When someone smiles at you, generally you smile back, don't you? Authentic leaders are not afraid to smile. They know that when they smile at team members, they create rapport and engagement. So, they smile often.

There are many types of smiles. When a person is comfortable with their smile and the teeth that show when smiling, they will generally smile broadly.

When someone is embarrassed about their teeth or self-conscious about their smile, they do not come across as strong as they could.

Authentic leaders are aware of their smile and share it often.

Step #6: Exercise

The older I get the more I value exercise. I find that with physical activity I feel better and look better. Perhaps my vanity is showing. When I do strength exercises my body feels more toned and this looks better to me. When I engage in cardiovascular exercises I know I increase my chances for longevity and reduce chances of heart problems and diabetes.

It is important to find an activity that you will do on a regular basis and do it, ideally at least three times a week for 30–60 minutes. Be sure to consider whether you prefer exercising alone or with other people. Do whatever inspires you to do it often.

Authentic leaders exercise their bodies. What are you doing?

Step #7: Mental Wellness

As I review my life it is clear to me that my level of mental wellness has been directly related to my level of wellness in other areas of my life. When I was challenged with *Candida albicans* and didn't know it, I was extremely confused and unhappy. When my diet was composed of fast food and heavy meat consumption, I was lethargic and lacked mental alertness. During the periods when I did not exercise regularly my focus was altered and I did not meet success as readily. I can see a clear connection throughout my life between my mental wellness and my success.

Mental wellness is a gift available to each of us. It starts with awareness of our self and our openness to other points of view. As humans we have the opportunity to make choices each and every day. The 'free will' that we are given leads us to a path of mental wellness or mental challenges. Our overall health begins with our attitude. You will rarely find an extremely healthy person who has a poor attitude. Positive attitudes breed health.

In my *Think – Communicate – Do* scenario, everything starts with the *Think* process. When your thoughts are positive you communicate positively and promote positive action. Thought is the place where mental wellness begins. You are in control of your thoughts and have the ability to create positive thoughts or negative ones. If your thoughts are negative, consider what that is doing to your life and your day-to-day activities.

Mental wellness is a matter of choice. You can choose to see the glass as half full rather than half empty. Maintaining mental wellness may require tweaking of your thoughts and lifestyle. It's worth the effort.

So much of mental wellness is attitude. Two people can look at the same situation and take away different perspectives based on their attitude. Sound mental health comes from a positive attitude. A positive attitude can be attained through thinking. Your responses to the statements that follow will help you to examine your thinking and the degree to which it is supporting or detracting from a positive attitude and sound mental health.

For the following ten questions, indicate the frequency to which these statements are true as follows: 5 = always, 4 = frequently, 3 = sometimes, 2 = seldom, 1 = never.

	5	4	3	2	1
I like myself.					
I am at peace with myself.					
I have eliminated self-destructive behaviors.					
I look forward to the future.					
I approach people with kindness.					
I speak well of other people.					
I don't hold grudges.					
I like to smile.					
I take myself lightly.					
Iaccept responsibility for the quality of my life.					

Look at your responses. Where do you see opportunities to modify your thinking to become more positive? How do you think that will impact your team?

Suggestions for maintaining positive mental health:

- Find humor in little things and promote humor in your environment.
- Laughter heals. It's easy to laugh; it's just a state of mind. Laugh often.
- If you can smile more often, you will attract more smiling, positive people.
- Remember that self-esteem is an attitude; it's your attitude about yourself.

Step #8: Natural vs. Chemical

Before ending this section, it is important that you gain a better understanding of the effects of chemicals on your overall wellness. Our bodies are not made of chemicals so when we put chemicals in and on our bodies we move our bodies out of their state of balance. Everything you put in, and on, your body affects your body.

Recently I had a hair analysis. This is when a lock of hair is analyzed to determine the level of metals that are in the body. The theory is that your hair holds on to those things that you have ingested over the past few months. The results of my hair analysis indicated that I needed to undergo a detox program to remove metals that had accumulated. I was quite surprised that the level of mercury in my body was high since I had recently done a chelation process after having the mercury fillings removed. This process of detox involved putting a foul-smelling liquid on my skin every other night. This process is called "transdermal" meaning that the medication entered my body through my skin. I would rub it in and it would do its thing.

This caused me to think about all the other things I have put on my body – lotions, deodorants, oils, chemical processes for my hair and more. If medication is applied by rubbing it on the skin then perhaps everything that is rubbed on the skin is ingested into the system through the skin. Very interesting. I thought about the lotions I had used in the past and their chemical ingredients. I also thought about the deodorants I had used – antiperspirants and other chemically based products. I also thought about the make-up that I use.

I began to read the labels of these products and noticed that they contained some of the metals that my hair analysis indicated I needed to remove – aluminum, bismuth, mercury, titanium – it's a long list. As a result, I have changed *all* my products to natural products. I purchase natural make-up at the health food store. It is made of plants and does not have chemicals. For deodorant I now use either crystals, homeopathics or naturally based deodorant. For lotion I use natural oils that I purchase from the health food store.

After being on this routine for about three years, I noticed that my skin was looking more vibrant. I continue to get healthier and people comment frequently about their positive view of my Outer Voice's Net Wellness. Taking the natural approach rather than blindly taking chemicals has been positive for me.

I have applied this approach to every other aspect of my health. I no longer take antibiotics or antihistamines. If I have a headache I drink catnip tea and/or take white willow, which is a naturally based, aspirin-type product. I have found a natural alternative to every chemical that I used to take in the past. I am better for it. My body is telling me clearly that it prefers the natural products to those that are chemically based. I have retained a positive balance of health, fitness and vitality and it is largely due to a conscious decision to use naturally based products. I am sure the same results will be evident for you.

As you go through the next week, look at every product that you put on or in your body. Read the ingredients. If there are chemicals included, consider investigating a change to natural products.

You can find natural products at the health food store closest to you. Also, you can search the Internet for natural products as well as uncovering extensive information about them. It will be to your advantage to do so.

Think – Communicate – Do

Most of us take our health for granted. This is particularly true when we are young. However, as we end each decade, we appear to become more concerned about our health. No matter what your age, you can take the steps needed to enhance your level of health and increase your longevity potential.

Think about the information that has been shared in this section. Revisit your comments and think about the type of wellness that you desire. Think about the modifications you will need to make in your life to attain the level of wellness that you desire.

Now do a little research by communicating your thoughts with others. Talk to friends and family and look at the Internet to learn all that you can. Prioritize your goals so that you know what steps you want to tackle first. As you *Communicate* with others learn from them and determine what is the healthiest way to move forward. Wait until you have clear direction before you move forward.

Once you are clear on your direction, take action with purpose. Make sure you have thought through your objectives and communicated potential paths. Once you make the decision and learn how to move forward, do so with assertive purpose and watch your health status improve beyond your dreams!

As your health status improves your personal strength and confidence will also improve. This will give your Outer Voice a boost, enabling you to lead with greater confidence and more smiles.

Case Study – *This case study is my story. I took antibiotics for 40 years for ear infections. This started before all the current literature about the challenges of antibiotics. In these 40 years I often took doses more than once a year and usually for the full cycle of ten days. Little did I know that this would cause a massive case of* Candida albicans, *a yeast infection that was creating an intricate web system throughout my organs. Over the years I've had 11 surgeries; most I attribute to the antibiotic use. At one point, I was getting infections every month and my body was way out of sync. My medical doctor prescribed multiple tests and declared me completely healthy, but I could not get out of the bed. I had no energy nor drive. I found a holistic doctor who was also a medical doctor and he treated me with multiple holistic and homeopathic remedies. It took a few years to clear the* Candida albicans *and other challenges. Without getting engaged in my Net Wellness needs and the authentic involvement of holistic and homeopathic perspectives, I do not believe I would be alive today.*

Authenticity Assessment Net Wellness Question

NET WELLNESS is defined as holistic wellness and balance.

Question: How balanced are your perspectives on wellness?
Response:

A. Score yourself 1 – 3 if your answer is "What does holistic mean?"

B. Score yourself 4 – 7 if your answer is "I understand my wellness needs and I'm making positive changes"
C. Score yourself 8 – 10 if your answer is "Holistic health principles are integrated in my life"

Circle your response:

1 2 3 4 5 6 7 8 9 10

Transfer the number you circled to Box #4 of the Your Authenticity Assessment Scores grid in Chapter 6.

Authentic leaders are energetic.

B. Network – Authentic Leaders Forge Quality Relationships

What Is Network?

There are three ways to look at Network.

The first is as the sum total of your relationships with people. The people you select to associate with speak volumes about how you understand yourself. There is a saying that goes, "Birds of a feather flock together." The people you 'flock' with give others an immediate impression about how you see yourself.

Life is made up of people. No one can escape this truth. No matter what your purpose, it involves other people. Who do you associate with? How large is your Network? How do you expand your Network? All of these are critical questions that relate to your Network. A quality Network creates a quality life. A Network of people who drain your energy weakens you.

The second way to look at Network is 'networking,' the act of connecting with other people. Networking is a popular tool to build your business and your Network. Going to various events, speaking about what you do, exchanging information with others, scheduling discovery conversations – these, and more, take place when you are networking.

The third way we look at Network is the net of your work, the sum total of the work you have done to get you to the point where you are now. Before you began your current work, you did something else in some type of work situation. Whether your work was a full-time job or as a full-time student, you gathered experience and memories that will have some impact on your future. The net of this work is what you bring to your current work situation.

Understanding and integrating these three Network perspectives is the sum total of your Network.

Part 1: Your Relationships with People

Success cannot be attained without the assistance of others. No leader is successful in isolation. The question to ask yourself is who do you have around you to talk to and to seek counsel and assistance from?

You basically have two different Networks of people around you. One is your quantity network and the other is your quality network.

Your quantity network is composed of people you have met but with whom you have not formed a close relationship. These are people you meet at networking events, they may be people at your workplace and others whose names are in your mobile phone but with whom you do not speak regularly. You don't know each other well; however, you are friendly.

On the other hand, your quality network is composed of those who know you well. This includes best friends, long-term friends, family and others who you mutually love, respect and trust. Quality network people will give you the truth. They know your faults and love you anyway.

Authentic leaders surround themselves with quality people and often seek their feedback. It's through quality networks that authentic leaders stay grounded because quality network give honest feedback and offer a barometer for growth. That's how a quality network helps the authentic leader be empowered. And when authentic leaders are empowered, they empower their teams.

You have three quality networks. Your family is your first quality network, since it is the one you were born into. This network of people helped to shape who you are. Your life began by imitating what these people did when they were in your presence. As you grew you began to question them as you learned different perspectives of life from new acquaintances. You also probably learned that your family extended beyond the people you lived with. You may have extended family in multiple parts of the world. Your family network is one that is often hard to escape.

Personal friends represent your second quality network. These are the people who you select to be a part of your life. They are people who you choose to contact and who you most enjoy being around. Often these chosen people are a part of your family.

Some members of your professional network may also be part of your quality network. These are people that you probably did not select but who were connected to you by the nature of your career. Self-employed people generally select the people that they work with. When you have a quality professional network you have access to people who can help you as an authentic leader.

Life always has more quality when your relationships are positive. I don't know anyone who is happiest when they are at odds with others. The statements on the next two pages will assist you to evaluate the quality of your Networks and how you build relationships with people.

The first group of statements represent behaviors – how you treat the people in your Network. For each statement, indicate the degree to which you agree with the statement: 5 = strongly agree, 4 = somewhat agree, 3 = neutral, 2 = somewhat disagree, 1 = strongly disagree.

	5	4	3	2	1
I have a circle of friends.					
I engage in activities with my friends.					
I listen when people speak to me.					
I return calls promptly.					
I give other people the benefit of the doubt.					
I support the ideas and interests of others.					
Friends enhance my life.					
I nurture new as well as longstanding relationships.					
I have both personal and professional friends.					
I share information freely.					
I don't judge others.					
I walk away from unhealthy relationships.					
I am my own best friend.					
There are people in my life who know my faults and love me anyway.					

Look at your responses and write your thoughts below:

____

____

____

____

____

This second group of statements represents your beliefs about people. For these statements indicate the degree to which you agree: 5 = strongly agree, 4 = somewhat agree, 3 = neutral, 2 = somewhat disagree, 1 = strongly disagree.

	5	4	3	2	1
Good communication builds strong teams.					
Really listening to someone means listening beyond the words.					
Being on good terms with someone means having mutual respect.					
Life is a community.					
Giving others the benefit of the doubt builds relationships.					
How we get along with other people says a lot about our level of peace, comfort and balance.					
To build relationships we must appreciate the ideas and interests of others and support and encourage them.					
Look for the good in each person with the concept that each of us is doing the best we can at any given moment.					
We must be our own best friend if we really expect our self-esteem to thrive.					

Examine your responses and draw your own conclusions. How do your responses align with the values you identified in the Integrity section? Do you see anything you need to tweak?

The quality of your Network speaks volumes about you. When people see you with your Network, what voice is spoken, what do your relationships say about you?

Which of the concepts in the previous pages are practiced within your team? Which could you role model to strengthen your team? Give thought to other modifications you can make based on your answers. How can you integrate some of the concepts within your team?

Part 2: Networking

Perhaps you have been to an event where some of the attendees ask you for your business card and/or shove their card in your hand without even engaging in a conversation.

You may not have any need or interest in the person or their services and will probably not contact them in the future, yet they force their card on you anyway. While this person may have gained a large network of contacts by collecting cards, without conversation, is this really a good way to network? If the goal is strictly to collect names of businesses, then it might work. But if the goal is to build relationships, this is probably not the best tactic. Networking is not just about passing out and collecting business cards. It's about building relationships. Authentic leaders build relationships.

All relationships start out in the quantity category, just another person you meet. Over time, some become quality relationships because they evolve into clients and/or friends. These relationships are generally built over time.

When I am networking, I set an intention. It is to get a small number of people to have interest in what I do. The fact that I have an intention to my networking is what drives success. One of the most effective ways I meet my intention is how I introduce myself, either to the entire group or to individual members.

Most people introduce themselves something like this: "Hi, here's my name and this is what I do or where I work. . . ." Then they may give a few accomplishments to get us to know about their credentials and successes. They may not realize that people care less about what you do and more about what you can do for them. Rather than introducing yourself with your credentials, let them know the value they will receive by connecting with you. This way you have pre-qualified the attendees and you know that if anyone begins to seek more information, they are interested in the value you bring them.

Let me give you an example. Rather than introducing yourself as a bank manager, perhaps you can introduce yourself by saying that you help people create a better future. Isn't that what happens when people manage their money effectively? That's what banks do, right? The person you are speaking with now may ask you how you help people create a better future, which gives you the opening to learn more about the person, their needs and then to educate them about how you can help them create a better future.

Once you are clear on the value that you bring, you can try different ways of explaining it to others. There is an authentic way for you to present it and you will know when you find it because of how people respond.

Here are some thoughts for enhancing your Network and becoming your own network coach. This may mean greater quantity and/or quality relationships. Your focus can be on family, professional and/or personal. Let's use the *Think – Communicate – Do* process to coach yourself.

Think

The guidelines on the next page relate to event networking and can also be applied to social media networking.

Consider the who, what, where, how and when of your networking.

WHO do you want to include in your Network? What type of people, from what backgrounds, doing what things? Who are these people, what are their objectives, what do they look like, what do they do, etc.?

WHAT will these people bring to you? Why do you want them in your Network? Why would they expand your Network? What will they do for you? What can you do for them?

WHERE can you meet these people? Will you need to go to business functions, parties, dancing, the theater, book signings, coffee shops, church, networking events, expos, talent shows, auditions, family reunions?

HOW will you approach them? Once you have put yourself in their presence you will have to develop an introductory statement that will enable you to establish rapport and build a relationship. How will you do that? What words will you say, what will you focus on, what is your objective, will you smile, extend a handshake, a hug? How will you bring these people into your world?

WHEN will you meet these people? Are you ready to go out and find them now, do you need to travel out of state, out of the country or are they around the block? Is your objective to expand your Network now or is your plan to be executed in another year or so?

Once you examine the characteristics of the people you want to meet you can refer to the person who has these characteristics as your 'avatar.' Your avatar is an imaginary person that represents your ideal client. What is your intention once you meet your avatar? Are you seeking leads, live appointments, discovery sessions? Know your intention and it will be easier to fulfill.

You now have a plan for networking. You know who you are looking for, where to find them, how to speak with them and the goal of the connection.

Communicate

Now it's time to *Communicate* your plan to determine its validity. Reflect on it, talk to others, modify, evaluate it, revise as needed and prepare to execute your plan. Create your introductory statement and begin practicing it. Identify your intention for networking.

What result do you want? Are you focused on quantity or quality? What value do you bring to the table? Practice your introductory statement on people who are close to you. Ask them for comments about how your statement flows, how comfortable you appear and how effective you might be. Modify as needed. Go out and *Communicate* to the world!

Do

Take all the information in the previous pages and develop a step-by-step plan of action to expand your Network. You will need to identify numerous outlets for

Network expansion. Identify the events you plan to attend, the objective of your involvement, when this will take place, where it will take place, the types of people you would like to meet, how you will evaluate your success and, after the event, the revisions you will make in your process to improve your success next time.

This is an excellent exercise to lead with your team. The collective input, especially with sales and customer service teams, could drive significant growth to your team.

Now you are ready to enhance the quality and quantity of your Network. The people that you meet will be glad that you did.

Authentic leaders Network authentically.

Part 3: Net of Your Work

Who you are today and what you bring to the table as a leader reflects all the work you have done in the past. It's all the jobs you have held, whether paid or not, the things you did in those jobs and what you liked and didn't like about them. The way your supervisors treated you and how you interacted with co-workers has impacted you in ways you might not even realize. There are probably some threads in these activities that can be found in the work you are doing now. All of these concepts are components of the third element of Network, which is the net of your work, the sum total of the work you have done. Authentic leaders learn from their experiences as they evolve to greater leadership capability.

Reflect on the work you have done in the past and how it impacts the work you do now. Ideally, you will reflect and write notes in your journal. Writing down your thoughts gives you the best opportunity to sort and learn from them.

Step #1: Think about all the jobs that you have held, whether paid or not. Set aside a time when you can spend an hour or even a full day (go to the beach, go fishing or just sit in your backyard) remembering your past. Go back as far as you can.

Step #2: Think about the things you did in these jobs. What were some of the activities that you liked? What did you not like?

Step #3: What are you doing now that is similar to what you did in the past? Are these things you like or dislike?

Step #4: What are the similarities/themes/threads that you see reflected in the net of your work? How do these similarities/themes/threads show up in your life now? Is there anything you need to change?

Step #5: How can you leverage what you learned about yourself to positively impact your current leadership role?

Authentic leaders build on their past and use those experiences and lessons to build the future. They especially learn from their past relationship experiences to build engaging relationships with people in their current networks.

Case Study *– Linda grew up in Los Angeles. Then when she married in her early 20s she moved to San Jose. She divorced after a few years of marriage but stayed in San Jose to raise her children. Once they were grown she moved back to Los Angeles to help take care of her ailing mother. When she returned she initiated a reunion with several of the ladies she went to high school with. Over the years she had maintained contact with these dozen ladies, so it was easy for her to collect these quality friends and bring them together. It's been 15 years and these ladies are still meeting for birthdays and an annual Christmas gathering. Linda's quality network also helped her over some challenging times with her mother's death and her entrepreneurial quests. In the process, she initiated new quantity relationships, some of which evolved into quality relationships. Linda has no regrets about any of her Networks.*

Authenticity Assessment Network Question

NETWORK is defined as the quality and quantity of your relationships.

Question: What do your associations say about you?
Response:

A. Score yourself 1 – 3 if your answer is "I do not have many friends"
B. Score yourself 4 – 7 if your answer is "I realize that if I enhance my associations I enhance my life"
C. Score yourself 8 – 10 if your answer is "I have high quality associations that benefit my growth"

Circle your response:

1 2 3 4 5 6 7 8 9 10

Transfer the number you circled to Box #5 of the Your Authenticity Assessment Scores grid in Chapter 6.

Authentic leaders build and role model quality relationships.

C. Net Wealth – Authentic Leaders Live with Joy

What Is Net Wealth?

Net Wealth is the sum total of your general contentment in life. When most people think of Net Wealth they immediately think of finances. From an authenticity perspective, Net Wealth refers to those things that bring abundance and joy. These could be relationships, family, knowledge, spirituality, freedom, and many other values that make you joyful. A person is wealthy when they live with joy.

When the leader is joyful, they role model joyfulness to their team. Even though we call our professions our 'work,' who says it has to feel like work? Why not promote a joyful culture when fulfilling the requirements of the job? When people live with joy they build community. Community builds rapport and creates long-term, loyal employees. This translates to less turnover and a joyful bottom line.

Wealth is something we all aspire to in one way or another. We at least seek financial comfort and elimination of financial struggle.

Let's look at wealth from a broader perspective. Isn't the quest for financial wealth also the quest for peace and contentment? Many of us feel that if we only had more money, we could purchase the things that would give us more contentment. We think of money as the means to an end, the means to obtaining those things that we feel will give us contentment.

But true contentment is not derived from money alone. It is a part of the equation, but it is not the entire equation. Many people have excess money, yet they are not happy. Others have little money yet sing gleefully every day. What makes the difference?

When wealth is viewed as money alone, it is a very narrow view of the world. It speaks in a voice that focuses strictly on material items, as if *things* are the secret to happiness. They are not.

The term Net Wealth refers to your collective wealth and is derived from an assessment of your overall understanding of the things that you have in abundance and the things that bring you joy and contentment. I know many people who are spiritually wealthy. They can call up unseen supporters at any moment and get instant results and their needs met. Others are relationship wealthy. They have friends who will do anything for them and who are the source of great contentment. Still others are wealthy in opportunity or generosity. Because they maintain such a positive attitude, you never know what challenges they are encountering – financial or otherwise. They don't let the challenges bother them and they inspire others just by being there.

What is the source of your wealth? Are you financially wealthy, spiritually wealthy, relationship wealthy, opportunity wealthy or do you excel in another area of wealth? Is your wealth balanced? If one area is stronger than the other, does it balance out your life so that you do not focus on the things that you don't have but instead focus on what you do have?

I have placed Net Wealth as a 'Do' on the Authenticity Grid because it is hard to gain wealth, of any kind, unless you 'do' something. Your financial perspective can often be seen by others in what you do on a daily basis – what you wear, the car you drive, where you live. It is also viewed based on how you conduct yourself when around others – do you express generosity, kindness and wisdom?

Authentic leaders understand broad definitions of wealth and role model joy for others to follow.

Authentic leaders also enhance the wealth of the organization. This is done not only with attention to the bottom line but also attention to the joy of their team members. When the team is content, it can flourish.

A leader can have a team of joyful employees even when there is some dissatisfaction with salary practices. This occurs when the team has shared values and the environment is engaging. The leader can create this by role modeling and by helping team members share a joyful mindset. Here are some ways to raise your Net Wealth.

Step #1: Take a Look at the ABC's of Authentic Wealth

These are areas where you have the potential to attain wealth. How can you, as the leader, model these traits?

ABC's of Authentic Wealth – An Abundance of:

Attitude
Brilliance
Collaboration
Determination
Effort
Focus
Gratitude
Humor
Ideas
Joy
Kindness
Loyalty
Mindset
Networking
Optimism
Patience
Questions
Resources
Self-Confidence
Trust
Understanding
Vitality
Wisdom
Xperience
Youthfulness
Zeal

Step #2: Assessment of Wealth

Do you feel that you and your team members are wealthy? Using the broadened definition of wealth, next to each one of the traits in the list that follows, identify the degree to which you feel you and your team have attained wealth in that area. Use the following scale:

> 5 = wealth attained, 4 = wealth near, 3 = wealth in process with more work, 2 = barely aware of this area, 1 = no movement in this area.

	You as Leader	Your Team
Attitude	______	______
Brilliance	______	______
Collaboration	______	______
Determination	______	______
Effort	______	______
Focus	______	______
Gratitude	______	______
Humor	______	______
Ideas	______	______
Joy	______	______
Kindness	______	______
Loyalty	______	______
Mindset	______	______
Networking	______	______
Optimism	______	______
Patience	______	______
Questions	______	______
Resources	______	______
Self-Confidence	______	______
Trust	______	______

Understanding	_______	_______
Vitality	_______	_______
Wisdom	_______	_______
Xperience	_______	_______
Youthfulness	_______	_______
Zeal	_______	_______
Add traits not listed:		
________________________	_______	_______
________________________	_______	_______
________________________	_______	_______
________________________	_______	_______
________________________	_______	_______
________________________	_______	_______
________________________	_______	_______
________________________	_______	_______

Step #3: Wealth Needs

List below those areas that you have marked as 3 or lower. These are the areas where you and/or your team could benefit from obtaining greater wealth. List them in order of 1's first, then 2's, then 3's for yourself and for your team.

Area	*Rank (#1 – 3)*	*Rank (#1 – 3)*
________________________	_______	_______
________________________	_______	_______
________________________	_______	_______
________________________	_______	_______
________________________	_______	_______
________________________	_______	_______
________________________	_______	_______
________________________	_______	_______

Do you and your team share any of the same traits that are scored at 3 or lower? These are areas to consider as a focus to increase the overall wealth of your team and you as their leader.

Now go back over your list and identify the five areas where you would most like to improve your wealth status, first for yourself, then for your team. Where do they connect? The area of connection represents your greatest need for a wealth attitude adjustment and to bring a more joyful attitude to your team.

Step #4: Methods to Achieve Needs – Think – Communicate – Do

To expand wealth even further, use the *Think – Communicate – Do* process.

Think

List the five areas you selected that represent areas where you would like to enhance your wealth status.

1. ____________________________ ____________________________
2. ____________________________ ____________________________
3. ____________________________ ____________________________
4. ____________________________ ____________________________
5. ____________________________ ____________________________

Consider why you have selected these five areas. Is it because you consider yourself in need in these areas or is your decision based on what other people have said to you? *Think* about this critically to assess your motivation for listing these five areas. Make sure that these are the five areas you want to address and be clear about your motivation for them. If they come from what others have said to you, examine if they are truly what *you* want. Sometimes we are greatly influenced by others without realizing it. When this happens, and we take action based on someone else's perception of our needs, we do not achieve contentment because we have based it on someone else's definition. Go back to your definition of wealth and make sure that the five areas that you have selected fall within your definition. If they don't, scratch out the one(s) you want to change and write the new area in the blank space to the right of your first choice.

Communicate

Conduct research to learn more about the five areas that you have selected. Go on the Internet and look up the definition of the words. Conduct a thesaurus analysis to find other words that mean the same. Talk to others to get their perceptions. Get team input. *Communicate* as many ways as you can to increase your understanding and broaden your perspective of your ability to attain abundance in the areas you have mentioned.

Do

Write an action plan or select a mini-team to write a plan that positions your team for extreme growth in one or two of these five areas. Start with just one or two, master them, then reassess. Success adjusting just one can positively impact one or more of the other four. Make sure your action plan will include things you will *Think* about, *Communicate* and *Do* in order to increase your effectiveness in each area. Your action plan should include, as a minimum, your objective, a timeline, activities, process for evaluation and a process for revision. Identifying a team to prepare the plan is an excellent way to get team member acceptance of the plan and increases the opportunity for success.

Keep in mind that the most important person who must find a joyful definition and practice of wealth is you, the authentic leader. To do so, there may be some changes you want to make.

Case Study – *Betty had a stellar career. She retired as the Vice President of Human Resources for an established national retail chain. After several months of a gnarling feeling within her, she made the decision one night and walked into her office in the morning and resigned. She walked out and has never looked back. But then she had to decide what to do next. She knew what she didn't want but wasn't sure what she did want. Next, she started coaching and also doing part-time work for her church. Once she was introduced to the nine dimensions of authenticity she felt she had found a new purpose in life. She made great money in her role as Vice President. But her satisfaction got lost in the culture of corporate competition that is common in so many corporate institutions. As she developed her practice using the nine dimensions of authenticity as her foundation, her abundance grew from personal growth and her ability to touch people in ways that are far more satisfying to her than what she could accomplish in her past. She is leveraging her past to thrive on her authentic path.*

Read Betty's experience in her own words in Chapter 10.

Authenticity Assessment Net Wealth Question

NET WEALTH is defined as abundance.

Question: How do you display your signs of wealth?
Response:

A. Score yourself 1 – 3 if your answer is "I lack abundance"
B. Score yourself 4 – 7 if your answer is "I understand broad abundance and am working on a plan to achieve"
C. Score yourself 8 – 10 if your answer is "I have abundance in many areas of my life"

Circle your response:

1 2 3 4 5 6 7 8 9 10

Transfer the number you circled to Box #6 of the Your Authenticity Assessment Scores grid in Chapter 6.

Authentic leaders are joyful.

D. Outer Voice Summary

Although authenticity begins in the Inner Voice, unless it is aligned with your Outer Voice, you probably do not come across as fully authentic. When you think of your Outer Voice, you want to have the confidence of knowing that your Inner and Outer Voices give the same message.

I've often spoken with people who say one thing, yet I clearly feel that there is a disconnect within them. It's like someone saying that they are very happy yet speaking it in very monotone, unexciting words and energy. Authenticity means that your Inner and Outer Voices match; they give the same message.

When someone looks at you, especially for the first time, they have no idea what is going on inside of you, they only know what they see. However, as you gain more familiarity with the concepts of authentic leadership you can assess yourself and whether your voices are giving the same message. You can do the same for your team members.

The ultimate goal is for the Inner, Outer and Expressive Voices to be in alignment. When you achieve that, you are perceived as extremely authentic in what you say and do. This also positions you to be the type of role model that others respect and want to work for.

Chapter 5

Expressive Voice Blueprint

Your Expressive Voice represents *who* you have become. It's how you do what you do in the world, how your Inner and Outer Voices are combined.

You express yourself in many ways. Each of the dimensions already discussed are ways to express yourself; however, they are subtle. Self-expression is both a subtle and an obvious activity. It's subtle because expression is often based on nuances, small things we do that we sometimes don't even realize we are doing. All of us get into a habit of using certain words and phrases, walking, talking and dancing in certain ways, as well as many other habitual things we do to express who we are.

We also do many obvious things, like standing up for a cause, allowing our personality to light up a room, appearing on stage or otherwise sharing our gifts with the world. The Expressive Voice is all about who you have become and how you position yourself for others to see you.

The Expressive Voice is the grown-up you who made conscious decisions to be somebody or do something. It's the fulfillment of your purpose and how you share it with the world. It stems from your Inner Voice and is supported or diminished by how people see you in your Outer Voice.

Authentic leaders are very clear about their Expressive Voice. They use their gifts and talents in the workplace and make opportunities for their team members to do the same. They know how to leverage their personality for the benefit of the team and the organization. And they have daily habits that support their perspective, position them for growth and enable them to be a solid role model for those who are watching.

The dimensions of the Expressive Voice are very deliberate ways of self-expression and include:

Legacy – defined as the natural gifts and talents you were born with. You received a unique set of gifts and talents that were given to us at birth. When we develop and use these gifts on a daily basis, we are happier and live more meaningful lives. Authentic leaders create empowering environments when they role model how to use natural gifts and talents in meaningful ways in the workplace.

Likeability – your personality and how you express it to the world. Authentic leaders know their best personality, share it often and help their team members do the same.

Lifestyle – your daily habits and how they support or detract from your authenticity. Authentic leaders are role models. This is an unwavering fact. How you live your life on a day-to-day basis greatly impacts the people who are watching you, which includes your entire team.

A. Legacy – Authentic Leaders Share Their Natural Gifts and Talents

What Is Legacy?

People generally think of the word 'legacy' in terms of what they will leave to their heirs. In our society we are taught to acquire things throughout our lifetime, which we can leave to our children and their children, to charities and others who have been meaningful to us in our lives.

From an authentic leadership perspective, Legacy refers to the gifts and talents you were born with. Each person receives a unique set of gifts and talents at birth that guide them to their authentic path on the planet.

What are your natural gifts and talents? How are you integrating them into your leadership style? Are you acknowledging the natural gifts and talents of your team members?

Authentic leaders share their natural gifts and talents with those whom they lead, and they allow those whom they lead to share their natural gifts and talents with each other. It's through our natural gifts and talents that long-term relationships are formed, and loyalty built.

When you recognize your employee's natural gifts and talents, acknowledge them. When possible, help employees integrate their natural gifts and talents into the work environment.

Likewise, integrate your own natural gifts and talents into the workplace. For example, if you have a verbal gift, hopefully your job includes speaking or writing. If you have a kinesthetic (movement) gift, hopefully you participate in the company's sports games, dancing or outings – or you initiate them.

If it's not possible to express your gifts at work, express them in other ways outside of the work environment. Expressing your natural gifts and talents is a way to maintain personal balance and life satisfaction and a great way of self-expression. When you understand your Legacy of gifts and talents, you improve your ability to express your authentic voice with confidence.

Being aware of your natural gifts and talents allows you to use them to create and develop positive circumstances in your life. This also leads you to operate your life with greater ease. With ease you remove unnecessary stress. This allows you to live in flow. When you are in flow you move closer to your purpose.

At the time of your birth you were gifted with attributes and talents that are unique to you and you alone. These gifts and talents give you a foundation for creating your life on earth. When you are aware of your special gifts and talents and use them accordingly, you are fulfilling your purpose and creating a more balanced life for yourself.

Your gifts are a unique combination of multiple intelligences, physical appearance, personality and character – all combining to create unique you. This combination of characteristics translates as your Legacy. How you combine them to create circumstances, events and opportunities becomes the voice of your Legacy.

If you were born with a gift in the arts and have a great affinity for landscape painting, you would probably not be in flow if you decide to work as an accountant. You will be a happier person, more aligned with your purpose and destiny and able to express yourself with greater ease if you pursue training in landscape painting and its related areas of specialty.

I'm reminded of my brother, who had a great affinity for playing the piano. He could hear a tune then sit at the piano and duplicate it. Yet my father did not feel that his son could make a living as a musician simply because others in his family had tried and not been successful. Therefore, my brother was put on a path of becoming a physician. It's no wonder that he rebelled at an early age and as a result never even completed college. He found his own way and often plays piano at blues clubs and is quite happy with it. He would have been miserable as a physician; that's not the area of his gifts.

What are your gifts? Are you using your gifts to your advantage or sweeping them under the rug with some notion that they have no value to you? Some people sweep them under the rug because they don't see how they can make a living expressing their gifts. Did you know that there are over 780 different industries within the United States? This means there is a minimum of 780 different areas in which you can make a living. Then within each of the 780 industries is a wide variety of jobs. Don't you think that your gifts and talents can fit into one of these 780 industries?

The blueprint that follows will assist you to examine your gifts and talents. You may be surprised by some of the areas that are defined as gifts. You will broaden your understanding and appreciation of gifts and get closer to understanding your authentic voice.

Building Your Legacy

In this section you will be able to examine the gifts you were born with and consider how the gifts are to assist you to strengthen your authentic voice. The gifts you will examine are divided into two categories – physical and wisdom gifts. To begin, we will look at your physical gifts.

Part 1: Physical Gifts

People don't often look at their physicality as a gift, but it is. Certain jobs are best suited for a certain body type, size, gender and other physical traits. For example, all basketball players are tall. Likewise, all gymnasts are small. Try putting a gymnast's body frame on the basketball court or a basketball player's body on the balance beam and it doesn't work well.

Physical gifts are obvious when people look at you. Many are traits that you have probably taken for granted or don't see as a gift at all. Most physical gifts cannot be changed. Although things in life are changing rapidly, you generally cannot change your height, skin color, gender or bone structure. These are gifts you were given at birth and your job is to use them well.

Yet so often we are unhappy with the gifts we were given. It's not unusual for people to undergo plastic surgery to change a nose, ears or other body parts. In fact, there is a steady increase of children, under the age of 18, who receive plastic surgery each year, up to a 300% increase. It's a changing value in our society. But most of us accept our body frame and make the best of it.

Authentic leaders accept who they are and their physicality. They do their best to maximize it by eating heathy, wearing appropriate clothes and otherwise honoring the body they were given. Authentic leaders also accept the physicality of their team members.

If you feel you need to increase your acceptance of your physical stature, consider this exercise:

Step #1: Stand in front of a mirror and look at yourself. First look at your face then at your entire torso. Examine the obvious things.

	Do you like?	
Describe your:	*Yes*	*No*
Chin shape:		
Ethnicity:		
Eye color:		
Face shape:		

(Continued)

Finger shape:		
Hair color:		
Hair texture:		
Hand size:		
Nose shape:		
Height:		
Legs:		
Lips:		
Nails:		
Physique (slim, average, heavy):		
Skin color:		
Shoe size:		
Teeth:		
Toes:		
Other:		
Other:		

Step #2: For each of the physical structures that you indicated you do not like, create a reason to embrace this gift that has been given to you. Look at the answers you wrote. Turn each of them into a positive statement of why you can like all aspects of the gift of your physical structure. Don't compare yourself with others. Just make a positive statement about each area that you listed:

____

____

____

____

____

____

____

____

Step #3: Your perception of your gifts is based on your thinking. Some people will spend a lot of energy agonizing about the shape of their nose and how they want it changed. Others with a similar nose shape will not be so affected. They will look at their nose shape and their attitude is one of gratefulness that their nose works adequately and provides the oxygen needed to fuel their body. Which attitude do you possess? Are you pleased with the physical gifts that were given to you or do you agonize over them?

Step #4: Identify five reasons you will embrace your physical gifts and feel proud. By doing so you enable your team members to do the same.

Part 2: Wisdom Gifts

You were born with numerous wisdom gifts that are expressed through the things that you do, what you say and how you act – your thoughts, emotions and behaviors. Wisdom gifts are very broad and often intangible.

Dr. Howard Gardner is the creator of the theory of multiple intelligences (MI theory). The essence of MI theory lies in honoring the unique giftedness of each person. It asserts that intelligence is a dynamic, ever-growing reality that can be expanded throughout one's life. Dr. Gardner defines intelligence as the ability to solve problems and to create products that are of value within one or more cultural settings.

Your multiple intelligences are gifts. According to Dr. Gardner, there are nine gifts of intelligence. Dr. Gardner does not refer to these as 'gifts'; I do. I refer to them as wisdom gifts because they are the seat of your wisdom, the way you learn and the way you express yourself. They also impact how you lead. These areas are:

- Visual/Spatial
- Musical
- Bodily/Kinesthetic
- Naturalistic
- Verbal/Linguistic
- Logical/Mathematical
- Interpersonal
- Intrapersonal
- Existential

On the following pages you will find nine brief inventories that address each of the wisdom gifts. Answer the questions to determine where your wisdom gifts lie. Look at each of the skills and determine if, based on your opinion, your ability is above average, average or below average.

After finishing each section, give yourself 3 points for every answer marked 'Above,' 1 point for every 'Average' and 0 for every 'Below,' then add the scores to get the total for that section.

Visual/Spatial

The ability to visualize an object and manipulate internal mental images/pictures. These individuals are gifted with sensitivity to color, shape, size, space, form and the relationship between these elements.

Look at each of the skills below and determine whether your ability is above average, average or below average.

	Above	*Average*	*Below*
Draws well.			
Likes to paint.			
Enjoys taking pictures with camera or video.			
Prefers books with pictures.			
Likes bright-colored clothes.			
Doodles.			
Is artistic.			
Can describe things in detail from memory.			
Shares vivid dreams.			
Likes puzzles and mazes.			
Is sensitive to color.			
Has a vivid imagination.			

Total responses ________ ________
x 3 x 1

Total for Visual/Spatial ________ + ______ = ______

Musical

The recognition of patterns, including various environmental sounds, and sensitivity to rhythm, pitch, tone and beat.

	Above	*Average*	*Below*
Hums frequently.			
Likes to sing.			
Creates music or songs.			
Plays an instrument or wants to.			
Easily remembers musical phrases.			
Likes to listen to music.			
Taps feet to music.			
Harmonizes easily to music.			
Can tell when notes are off key.			
Puts lessons to song or music.			
Seems to feel music.			
Beats rhythms.			

Total responses ________ ________

x 3 x 1

Total for Musical ________ + ________ = ______

Bodily/Kinesthetic

Physical movement (coordination, dexterity, balance, strength, flexibility, etc.) and the knowing/wisdom of the body.

	Above	*Average*	*Below*
Has difficulty standing still.			
Sometimes thinks they have ADD/ADHD.			
Enjoys physical activity.			

(Continued)

Likes to touch different things to get the feel of them.			
Uses hands to talk.			
Is very active.			
Taps pencils, foot, fingers.			
Appears to be well-coordinated.			
Likes to be busy doing something.			
Enjoys playing sports.			
Engages in physical activity to work out problems.			
Likes to work with hands.			

Total responses	_______ x 3	_______ x 1	
Total for Bodily/Kinesthetic	_______ +	_______ =	_______

Naturalistic

The ability to think and learn through nature.

	Above	*Average*	*Below*
Likes being outdoors.			
Shows respect for nature.			
Likes nature TV programs.			
Paints nature pictures.			
Enjoys books about science.			
Collects insects.			
Likes animals.			
Digs in dirt (or did when younger).			
Picks up bugs – dead or alive.			
Likes hiking.			

(*Continued*)

Collects flowers, shells and nature items.			
Can identify different birds, flowers, animals.			

Total responses ______ ______

x 3 x 1

Total for Naturalistic ______ + ______ = ______

Verbal/Linguistic

The ability to effectively use words and language, both written and spoken.

	Above	*Average*	*Below*
Talks a lot.			
Has a broad vocabulary.			
Asks a lot of questions.			
Started talking earlier than other children.			
Is interested in books.			
Likes to read or be read to.			
Reads stories and/or selects books eagerly.			
Enjoys word games.			
Easily remembers stories/tells stories in own words.			
Likes to rhyme/poetry.			
Is articulate.			
Tells/writes original stories.			

Total responses ______ ______

x 3 x 1

Total for Verbal/Linguistic ______ + ______ = ______

Logical/Mathematical

Inductive and deductive thinking/reasoning, numbers and the recognition of abstract patterns.

	Above	*Average*	*Below*
Likes numbers.			
Finds math easy.			
Counts things.			
Likes to solve problems.			
Sequences easily.			
Likes puzzles.			
Wants to know how things work.			
Is a good math student.			
Likes connecting dot games.			
Approaches things logically.			
Finds a rational explanation for most things.			
Notices patterns in things.			

Total responses ________ ________

x 3 x 1

Total for Logical/Mathematical ________ + ________ = ______

Interpersonal

Understanding and perceiving the motivations, moods, needs and feelings of other people.

	Above	*Average*	*Below*
Gets along well with others.			
Has several close friends.			
Likes to be involved in social organizations.			

(*Continued*)

Often thinks differently than others.			
Is a leader.			
Likes crowds.			
Likes teamwork.			
Moves easily between groups.			
Doesn't like to be alone.			
Is friendly.			
Prefers team sports to those requiring individual effort.			
Always wants friends around.			

Total responses ________ ________

x 3 x 1

Total for Interpersonal ________ + ________ = ________

Intrapersonal

Inner states of being, self-reflection, and awareness of spiritual realities. It is the ability to act on knowledge of self (inner moods, feelings, motivations, intentions, desires).

	Above	*Average*	*Below*
Likes to be alone.			
Is independent and strong-willed.			
Likes to work with or help people.			
Keeps a diary or journal.			
Likes solitary games and activities.			
Is sensitive.			
Is shy.			
Does not draw attention to self.			
Is reflective and meditative.			
Is quiet.			

(*Continued*)

Would prefer a more rural than urban environment.			
Seems to think deeply.			

Total responses ________ ________

x 3 x 1

Total for Intrapersonal ________ + ________ = ________

Existential

Sensitivity and capacity to tackle deep questions about human existence, such as the meaning of life, why we die, and how we got here.

	Above	*Average*	*Below*
Frequently ponders the meaning of life.			
Feels a special connection to unseen energies.			
Recognizes a shared identity with others.			
Wonders "why do we die?" and/or "how did we get here?"			
Feels like an 'old soul.'			
Has a sixth sense/is highly intuitive/psychic.			
Has past life memories.			
Communicates with animals.			
Feels connected to other planets.			
Curious about consciousness.			
Is aware of multiple realities.			
Has interest and capacity to tackle big questions about life.			

Total responses ________ ________

x 3 x 1

Total for Existential ________ + ________ = ________

Part 3: Scoring

After finishing each section list your gifts below, putting the gifts with the highest score on top and the lowest score on bottom.

Based on this inventory, my wisdom gifts, beginning with the most dominant (the category with the highest score) appear to be in this order:

Gift (Most Dominant First)	*Score*

Ask yourself, how are you using your gifts in your workplace? Authentic leaders are very aware of their wisdom gifts and use them in their leadership role. For example, if their gift is verbal they strengthen their communication skills, so that they connect most effectively with their team members. If their gift is interpersonal they use this gift to bring people together.

In addition, authentic leaders recognize the wisdom gifts of their team members. As we move into the Empowerment Age, this area of Legacy becomes increasingly important. Those entering the workforce in the Empowerment Age want their work to be connected to their gifts. For example, someone with an interpersonal gift would not be placed in a solitary job that does not have contact with others. You want someone with interpersonal abilities to be in front of your customers and clients sharing the wisdom about the work through their personality. It is becoming increasingly important to place people based on their gifts because this also means they will have more meaning in their work. Having a meaningful career also leads to greater loyalty simply because people enjoy doing what comes easy to them and what is aligned to their view of their purpose in life. Since gifts and talents come naturally and people enjoy what comes naturally, consider employing people in the area of their gifts. This is especially true in the Empowerment Age because most of the careers that many of the Empowerment Age employees will engage in have not been developed yet.

- What are your thoughts about your physical gifts? Wisdom gifts?
- Do they complement each other?
- Are you using your gifts in your life now?

Take some time and consider what you are thinking. Try to think between the thoughts so you can get to your authentic feelings. Journal your thoughts. Feel free to give yourself the gift of positive attitude.

Look at your list of wisdom gifts and your comments about your physical gifts. Consider where your strongest gifts lie. Don't look at the numbers you scored, look within yourself. List your gifts, putting the strongest first descending to the weakest gift.

My Greatest Gifts

In the space below, list your most dominant gifts:

(Continued)

Look at your long list and congratulate yourself for your uniqueness. Over the next few days or weeks, think about this long list of gifts that you possess. Ask yourself how you are sharing your gifts with the world. Are you only sharing a few gifts? Do you see some gifts that you didn't even know that you had? Are there some gifts you want to develop?

Now that you know your gifts you can create circumstances, events and opportunities for your gifts to shine. The Network section can provide suggestions for exposing your gift to others. The Intuition section can assist you to access your Inner Voice and receive direction on the use of your gifts. Remember, you were given the gifts for a reason – to fulfill your purpose and meaning in life. Access your Inner Voice and listen to inner instructions on how to move forward with your gifts. When you are able to 'hear' your Inner Voice give direction you will be in touch with your authentic voice.

Think – Communicate – Do

Take time and think about the gifts you were given. They are yours for a reason and can provide a vital link to fulfilling your purpose. Use your intuitive nature to gain more understanding of your gifts and how you are to use them. Consider yourself blessed to have the gifts that you do.

Share your gifts with others. They weren't given to you to hoard selfishly or hide.

Are you using all of your gifts? They were given to you to use. Unless you do something with them you may lose them.

Case Study *– Dexter is familiar with all of the dimensions, yet Legacy is his favorite one. Born in the Caribbean, Dexter was not made aware of many of the concepts that are shared in the Legacy dimension. Once he learned them, he came to realize that his decision to become a naturopathic physician was grounded in the gifts and talents he expressed as a child. He always had an interest in energy and how certain herbs can impact health. But he didn't really know himself. Once he began to delve into his natural gifts and talents, an entire new world opened up for him. He made a better assessment of his authentic path, tweaked a few things and has emerged as a significant contributor to the wellness of others just by sharing his true self. Dexter has a quote about what he has learned from the nine dimensions of authenticity, "I don't know where I can get this level of understanding on any program that I've ever been with. It's metaphysical, psychological, ecological, spiritual, intellectual and everything else. I love it!"*

Read Dexter's experience in his own words in Chapter 9.

Authenticity Assessment Legacy Question

LEGACY is defined as the degree to which you recognize and utilize your natural gifts and talents.

Question: Are you using your gifts in ways to communicate with the world?
Response:

A. Score yourself 1 – 3 if your answer is "What natural gifts and talents?"
B. Score yourself 4 – 7 if your answer is "I am aware of them and wondering how to use them"
C. Score yourself 8 – 10 if your answer is "I have integrated my gifts and talents in my life"

Circle your response:

1 2 3 4 5 6 7 8 9 10

Transfer the number you circled to Box #7 of the Your Authenticity Assessment Scores grid in Chapter 6.

Authentic leaders honor natural gifts and talents and those of their team members.

B. Likeability – Authentic Leaders Are Likeable

What Is Likeability?

Likeability refers to your personality, the behavior and energy you share with others. It is the sum total of your emotion, thought and behavior patterns and how they are expressed to the outside world. Your Likeability plays an important role in how you express yourself and how others relate to you. Likeability can give you entry into new people and places and plays an important role in your authentic expression of self.

We have one basic personality and many different ways to express it. The authentic leader recognizes that these personalities are part of the leadership role. Sometimes your team needs to experience your most serious side because getting the work done is serious business. Sometimes the team needs your humorous personality because levity breaks the routine. Occasionally team members may need the nurturing side of your leadership style and other times the disciplinarian.

Being adaptable to different ways of expressing yourself increases your authenticity and your strength as a leader. Leading from the likeable aspects of your own authentic personality is the key.

While your Outer Voice is how people perceive you, the Expressive Voice of likeability is how you express yourself to others. When you are likeable, people are more apt to be responsive to you.

We learn to be likeable when we are young children. When we see how others react to us as we talk or take action, we learn to adapt our behaviors to fit the situation. By the time we become adults we have established a pattern of behaviors that express our emotions and thoughts and become our personality.

Some personalities are likeable, and some are not. Aren't you more attracted to people who have pleasant personalities rather than those who do not? Isn't it easier to deal with someone who is likeable than someone who is not? Don't you find that [illegible] to you when you are in a more likeable frame of mind than when you are not? Then isn't it reasonable that you will be a more effective leader when you are likeable than when you are not?

With knowledge about how likeable you are to others you will be equipped to modify your personality to express yourself in a more likeable manner.

I went to a seminar recently where leadership was discussed. One of the CEOs of a major bank was part of a panel and he shared that he has known another CEO whose style of leadership is to see how often he can make employees, particularly women, cry. His barometer for a successful day was how many people he could make cry. A year later he was fired. His leadership attitude may have worked to some degree in the Industrial Age, but in today's world, the priority is helping employees be content and engaged in the workplace and not fearful.

Finding Your Likeability

You will examine your Likeability factor by looking at your personality and assessing how others react to your natural nature as well as your developed nature. All personality is a combination of the natural energy combined with the modification of the energy based on human experience.

Step #1: How You See Yourself – Self-Questionnaire

The "How you see yourself" self-questionnaire is a list of personality traits. Go through the list and indicate whether, in your opinion, your expression of this trait is not enough, just right or too much.

	Need to Be More	*Just Right*	*Need to Be Less*
Accountable			
Agreeable			
Amiable			

(Continued)

Assertive			
Assured			
Authoritative			
Bold			
Builds relationships			
Calm			
Competent			
Confident			
Conscientious			
Creative			
Deliberate			
Dominant			
Easygoing			
Egocentric			
Emotionally stable			
Emphatic			
Energizing			
Extroverted			
Flexible			
Giving			
Gregarious			
Helping			
Imaginative			
Impulsive			
In control			
Mild-mannered			
Natural			

(*Continued*)

Open			
Orderly			
Positive			
Private			
Rule-conscious			
Self-aware			
Self-disciplined			
Sensitive			
Socially bold			

Step #2: How Others See You

Now take this same list and have four people from your quality network complete it. Consider a family member, friend, co-worker, significant other, child, neighbor, business associate, church member or someone else who interacts with you enough to have an opinion in these areas. Feel free to share with more than four people to get a broader view of how you are perceived. Having both personal and professional contacts give feedback will be very helpful.

Ask each person to complete this spontaneously rather than taking time to think about each trait. Generally, the first answer that comes to mind is the most appropriate. Longer considerations are frequently a way of trying to give you the answer that they think you want rather than the answer that is most authentic to them. There is a copy of the questionnaire here, which you can copy to send to your selected people.

To____

On the following pages is a list of personality traits. Go through the list and indicate whether, in your opinion, my expression of this trait is not enough, just right or needs to be more for each trait.

	Need to Be More	*Just Right*	*Need to Be Less*
Accountable			
Agreeable			
Amiable			
Assertive			
Assured			
Authoritative			
Bold			
Builds relationships			
Calm			
Competent			
Confident			
Conscientious			
Creative			
Deliberate			
Dominant			
Easygoing			
Egocentric			
Emotionally stable			
Emphatic			
Energizing			
Extroverted			
Flexible			
Giving			

(Continued)

Gregarious			
Helping			
Imaginative			
Impulsive			
In control			
Mild-mannered			
Natural			
Open			
Orderly			
Positive			
Private			
Rule-conscious			
Self-aware			
Self-disciplined			
Sensitive			
Socially bold			

Step #3: Examine Differences/Similarities

On the following questionnaire, record your responses in the first column using a red marker. Then use a black pen to record the responses of each of the four (or more) people who responded.

	You	*#1*	*#2*	*#3*	*#4*
Accountable					
Agreeable					
Amiable					
Assertive					
Assured					
Authoritative					
Bold					
Builds relationships					
Calm					
Competent					
Confident					
Conscientious					
Creative					
Deliberate					
Dominant					
Easygoing					
Egocentric					
Emotionally stable					
Emphatic					
Energizing					
Extroverted					
Flexible					
Giving					

(Continued)

Gregarious					
Helping					
Imaginative					
Impulsive					
In control					
Mild-mannered					
Natural					
Open					
Orderly					
Positive					
Private					
Rule-conscious					
Self-disciplined					
Self-reliant					
Sensitive					
Socially bold					

Now look at the results on the questionnaire. Take some time and examine them. Do you see any patterns? How much do your responses mirror those of your associates? Do you see yourself as others see you? Consider writing comments in your journal.

Step #4: Examine Yourself

When you look at the totality of the assessments, do you have an abundance of traits that are similar? For example, many traits could be considered assertive or many traits could be considered mild-mannered. Do you and the people you selected rate you similarly in each of these? Do you feel that there are areas in your personality that you need to modify? Do you need to become more likeable? Do you need to modify emotions, thoughts and/or behaviors?

Think – Communicate – Do

Are you happy with your personality? Do you think you can change it? You can!

What you *Think* becomes your reality. A few years after I started the speakers' bureau, I questioned how I could have more success. I realized that as far as personality, I was equally introverted as extroverted. I was introverted because I love alone time. That's where I think, evaluate, assess and write. I am very creative when my introverted self shines. Then, when I am around people, especially when I am speaking, training, coaching or consulting, I am very extroverted.

After I wrote this program (using my introverted side) I realized that introverted energy would not allow me to successfully market my speakers, myself or my products. I decided that I would be more successful if I was just a little more extroverted. I started to 'think' about the personality traits I could modify or adapt to be more extroverted. As a result, I 'tweaked' myself to bring out my extroverted side. In a few months I acquired the extroverted edge I was seeking. You can *Think* your way to a personality change too.

By understanding my personality and aligning it with the other eight dimensions of my authentic voice, I am more authentic, and I am increasing my success in life. I *Communicated* my desire to become more extroverted to my closest friends. We talked about what this would mean and how they could help me. As I modified my personality my friends were my guidepost, letting me know which modifications best complimented me.

The activities I engaged in as I modified my behavior allowed me to *Do* things slightly differently than I had before. The result – I used the *Think – Communicate – Do* process to become more extroverted and this tweaking of my personality has helped me become more successful.

You can modify your personality too.

***Case Study** – When I met Peggy, she was a nurse who was starting a journey of becoming a professional speaker. Peggy approached me with a very quiet personality as she shyly told me of her desire to become a speaker. As I worked with Peggy I began to see variations of her personality that were not evident when we first met. Through the process of aligning with her authentic path, she started speaking and sharing information on how important it is to take care of your heart – both physically and emotionally. Before long Peggy spoke at an event and received a standing ovation. I was one of the ones in the audience standing for her. By stepping into what she knew she wanted to do, getting training to do it right, raising her confidence level, she emerged with the most charming, inspiring and natural personality, which draws people to her message and leaves them wanting more. Peggy shares this authentic part of herself and lives with great joy that she stepped out of her comfort zone and became the speaker she has always dreamed of being.*

Read Peggy's experience in her own words in Chapter 8.

Authenticity Assessment Likeability Question

LIKEABILITY is defined as your personality.

Question: What does the person you expose to the world say to the world about who you are?

Response:

A. Score yourself 1 – 3 if your answer is "I didn't know I could modify my personality"
B. Score yourself 4 – 7 if your answer is "I recognize my personality pros and cons"
C. Score yourself 8 – 10 if your answer is "I have modified my personality to reflect my best self"

Circle your response:

1	2	3	4	5	6	7	8	9	10

Transfer the number you circled to Box #8 of the Your Authenticity Assessment Scores grid in Chapter 6.

Authentic leaders are likeable.

C. Lifestyle – Authentic Leaders Have a Lifestyle of Beneficial Habits

What Is Lifestyle?

Lifestyle refers to your expression of attitudes, tastes, moral standards, economic level and mode of living through your habits. It's the way you live your life on a day-to-day basis. Your Lifestyle is an outward reflection of what you think, and how you communicate. Examining your Lifestyle helps you understand where you place your emphasis and how you are using your energy through the habits that you have established.

Authentic leaders approach discipline from two perspectives. The first perspective is the habits and behaviors that enable peak performance. Authentic leaders are role models for attendance, good work habits, meeting deadlines, respect, work ethics and a host of other qualities that support the work to be done.

Equally important is the second perspective, the leader's relationship habits. These are behaviors that build rapport and loyalty among team members. These behaviors include greeting employees, acknowledging work well done, celebrating success, caring, asking about family members and taking advantage of opportunities to get to know team members beyond the job.

By combining these two aspects of discipline, authentic leaders offer a work experience where employees care about each other. This is an engagement-building aspect of the leadership experience.

Our Lifestyle is reflected in the choices that we make. A healthy Lifestyle is reflected through healthy choices. When you interact with people they gain a sense of your Lifestyle by how they see you living your life – not only the clothes you wear and car that you drive, but also by the things they hear you say, and see you do. The things you do are generally reflected in your habits. We create habits throughout our lives. Sometimes they become so routine that we run on autopilot, forgetting when or why we created the habit and thus, the Lifestyle that we are living.

In this section you will have the opportunity to look at yourself through the habits that you engage in and to consider modifying your Lifestyle accordingly.

Have you thought about the Lifestyle you are living? Do you move around your day in a full state of consciousness about what you are doing or are you just repeating habits in a meaningless way?

Your Lifestyle is an important expression of yourself and is the final segment of the nine dimensions of authenticity. You express yourself through your Lifestyle, the sum total of all of your thoughts, communications and actions. It is the last section and it reflects all previous sections.

You are going to examine your Lifestyle by looking at your habits. Your habits are an expression of your gifts and personality. You can change or tweak a negative habit to turn it into a positive habit that serves your purpose of achieving your authentic voice. The process to do this involves identifying the habit, making the decision to modify it, creating an alternative habit and then incorporating the new habit into your Lifestyle. This is similar to the idea that your thoughts create your reality. In the same way that your thoughts create your reality, your habits create your outcome.

Creating Authentic Habits

Step #1: Identifying Habits

You will spend one full day examining your habits. Select a day in the near future when you will be engaged in your normal activities and have the opportunity to take thoughtful notes. Try to make notes at least every hour, reflecting on not only what you *Did* but also what you *Thought* about. You can also include what you *Communicated* to someone else using the guidelines on the next page. Then indicate whether the habit supports or takes away from your authentic voice and how you express yourself to the world. You can use your phone to audio record your activities for the day then transfer the activities to your journal. Record the *activities* you engaged in, your *thoughts* at the time and what you *communicated* in each of the following parts of your day:

- One hour after you get up
- Transportation to work/school
- Activities at work/school
- Mid-morning
- Activities at work/school
- Lunch

- Activities at work/school
- Mid afternoon
- Activities at work/school
- Transportation from work/school
- Home arrival
- Dinner
- After-dinner activities
- Preparation for bed

Other activity not listed____

Another activity not listed____

After completing your list for the day, review it and decide if each of your notations reflect positive, negative or neutral attitudes. Applaud yourself for your positive habits and use the next step to turn the negative habits into positive ones.

Step #2: Modifying Habits

List your negative habits in the grid on the next page on the left side. On the right side, brainstorm alternate activities, thoughts or ways to communicate that you can create to tweak or completely change the negative habits to positive ones. For example, one of my past habits was in the *communicate* area when I would tell myself that I could have done a better job each time I spoke in public. I wrote this on the left side. On the right side I wrote, "I always do my best when I'm on stage."

Another habit that I modified was eating bread. I love warm rolls with butter and sometimes would toast bread in the morning. Then I noticed that I was gaining weight and that was basically because I do not digest bread well. My new habit is to only eat bread when I am at a restaurant. Since I only eat at restaurants about twice a month, this enables me to still enjoy warm bread but in a way that is healthy for me.

One more example is driving. Since I work at home I have a lot of control of when I am driving. Occasionally I have to drive during rush hour and one day I sat through five lights to go one block. My patience just doesn't do well with this and my hat goes off to those who do it on a daily basis. For me though, to keep my patience intact and not get stressed, I downloaded a new app that directs me to side streets to bypass crowded traffic and my new habit is to use that app whenever I feel stressed in traffic. Next time I will also give myself the option of audio to listen to.These modifications have helped me to increase my patience, reduce my stress, provide more productive time and keep me happier. As you write your habits, consider how your life can be more joyful with just a few habit tweaks.

Negative Habit	*Modified Habit*

Step #3: Patterns of Negative Habits

Review the list of negative habits that you have now changed to positive. As you review the list, see if you find any patterns that give you more insight on how you could benefit from modifying your Lifestyle, then list the patterns in the grid on the next page. For example, are there negative habits that only reveal themselves when you are at home? Are your habits related to fulfilling time schedules? Is there a relationship to any person or people in your life? Do the negative habits reveal themselves only on the job? Is there a pattern that shows up during transportation times? Take time and evaluate any patterns, then list them on the next page. Indicate whether it is a *Think*, Communicate or Do activity. This will guide you if you evaluate tweaking your thoughts, communication or behavior.

Identified Pattern	*T-C-D*	*When It Shows Up*

Step #4: Examine Yourself

Now go over the list of patterns and evaluate whether it is a habit of thought, communication or action. To the right of each habit that you identified, put either a T (*Think*), C (*Communicate*) or D (*Do*).

Results:

Number of *Think* patterns ______________

Number of *Communicate* patterns ______________

Number of *Do* patterns ______________

Now you can examine the source of your negative patterns and modify them based on their source.

Step #5: Incorporating New Habits to Create a New Lifestyle

Think – Communicate – Do

If you need to tweak your *Thinking* habits, go back and complete the *Think* exercises, which you can find on the three first sections in each chapter that begin with (A).

If you need to tweak your *Communication* habits, review the exercises on the second section of each chapter that begin with (B).

If you need to tweak your *Do* habits, re-examine the exercises on the third section of each chapter that begin with (C).

A properly tweaked Lifestyle provides opportunity for longevity. When you tweak your *Think – Communicate – Do* habits to accommodate your purpose, you have created an environment that will lead you to your greatest capability to achieve.

Case Study *Diana was ready to retire as a female sales manager in the male-dominated beer industry. As a child, Diana made the decision to not get married nor have children because she did not like the way it had turned out for her mother. So when she decided to retire she had no idea what to do with herself. She learned about the nine dimensions of authenticity and uncovered the path she wanted to follow in her retirement years. She changed her Lifestyle to meet with senior citizens to assist them. In the process, she learned that they did not have access to farm fresh food so she started a non-profit to deliver farm fresh food to the retirement homes where seniors lived. This grew to a citywide business that is now supported by major corporations.*

Authenticity Assessment Lifestyle Question

LIFESTYLE is defined as your day-to-day habits.

Question: How do your habits speak to who you are?

Response:

A. Score yourself 1 – 3 if your answer is "I have habits?"
B. Score yourself 4 – 7 if your answer is "I am aware of habits that I need to change and I'm ready to address them"
C. Score yourself 8 – 10 if your answer is "My habits enhance my life"

Circle your response:

1 2 3 4 5 6 7 8 9 10

Transfer the number you circled to Box #9 of the Your Authenticity Assessment Scores grid in Chapter 6.

Authentic leaders role-model good habits.

D. Expressive Voice Summary

How you express yourself is a huge part of your authenticity because it's what separates you from others in tangible ways. Your Inner Voice separates you from others; however, no one knows what another person's inner voice is saying so it's an intangible separation. This makes it difficult to validate how you may be aligned with another person's Inner Voice unless you engage in conversation, sometimes lengthy conversation.

When two people walk into a room wearing the same outfit there is an immediate Outer Voice connection. When I've seen someone wearing what I am wearing I tell them that they have good taste. We make an instant connection that seldom goes farther than the acknowledgement of what we are wearing. I have never built a quality authentic relationship in this manner, not even a quantity relationship.

But connect two people who have the same Expressive Voice wisdom gift and sparks may fly. There is a certain affinity with people who have the same gifts. Writers love to connect with other writers and people who express themselves with words. Kinesthetic dancers and athletes always gather together. Artists have their own communities, and so on. When you meet other people who express themselves in the world in ways that you do, a strong bond is often made.

This is the power of the Expressive Voice. Knowing the power gives authentic leaders a clue to leadership, a very important clue that can make a major difference in how you lead and the success of your team. This is also the power of the upcoming Empowerment Age and the secret sauce to engagement in the Empowerment Age that adds meaning and commitment to team members.

Once you are able to align your team members' roles with their natural gifts and talents, so that their time at work helps them grow, develop and/or express their gifts, you have found a reliable way to maximize your authenticity as a leader.

This would be you being authentic and helping your team members to do the same. Authenticity has a lot to do with individuality. As an authentic leader, your role is the delicate balancing act of bringing out the individuality of each team member, guiding them to be authentic in their individuality and creating opportunities for them to integrate their authentic individuality into your team assignments. Not an easy task but one that can be accomplished with patience and a plan.

The case studies that follow will help you understand the Authenticity Grid in new ways and learn of the experiences of others who have used the concepts of the Authentic Voice System to impact their work environment. The greatest value you will receive is to implement the concepts in your workplace. If you would like to discuss the possibilities, please reach out to us at 323-734-7144 or email Coaching@NormaHollis.com.

Chapter 6

Scoring the Authenticity Assessment

Now you have the information you need to assess how authentic you are on your path to become an authentic leader. To begin, you will determine your level of authenticity by calculating your score for the responses you made for each dimension of authenticity.

You should have transferred your responses for each of the Authenticity Assessment scores to the chart on the next page. If you have not, go back to each section's question and transfer your answer to the chart on the next page.

Box #1 – Intuition, answer to Authenticity Assessment Intuition Question
Box #2 – Integrity, answer to Authenticity Assessment Integrity Question
Box #3 – Inspiration, answer to Authenticity Assessment Inspiration Question
Box #2 – Net Wellness, answer to Authenticity Assessment Net Wellness Question
Box #2 – Network, answer to Authenticity Assessment Network Question
Box #2 – Net Wealth, answer to Authenticity Assessment Net Wealth Question
Box #2 – Legacy, answer to Authenticity Assessment Legacy Question
Box #2 – Likeability, answer to Authenticity Assessment Likeability Question
Box #2 – Lifestyle, answer to Authenticity Assessment Lifestyle Question

A. Your Authenticity Assessment Scores

	INNER VOICE	OUTER VOICE	EXPRESSIVE VOICE	TOTAL
THINK	BOX #1 INTUITION _______	BOX #4 NET WELLNESS _______	BOX #7 LEGACY _______	_______ X
COMMUNICATE	BOX #2 INTEGRITY _______	BOX #5 NETWORK _______	BOX #8 LIKEABILITY _______	_______ Y
DO	BOX #3 INSPIRATION _______	BOX #6 NET WEALTH _______	BOX #9 LIFESTYLE _______	_______ Z
TOTALS	_______ A	_______ B	_______ C	_______ X + Y + Z + _______ A + B + C

Steps to calculate your score:

1. Add the numbers vertically in Boxes 1 + 2 + 3. Put the sum in Box A. This is your score for INNER VOICE.
2. Add the numbers vertically in Boxes 4 + 5 + 6. Put the sum in Box B. This is your score for OUTER VOICE.
3. Add the numbers vertically in Boxes 7 + 8 + 9. Put the sum in Box C. This is your score for EXPRESSIVE VOICE.
4. Add the numbers horizontally in Boxes 1 + 4 + 7. Put the sum in Box X. This is your score for THINK.
5. Add the numbers horizontally in Boxes 2 + 5 + 8. Put the sum in Box Y. This is your score for COMMUNICATE.
6. Add the numbers horizontally in Boxes 3 + 6 + 9. Put the sum in Box Z. This is your score for DO.
7. Add your vertical scores (A + B + C) and put in the bottom right box on the appropriate line.
8. Add your horizontal scores (X + Y + Z) and put in the bottom right box on the appropriate line.
9. Add these two scores (A + B + C) + (X + Y + Z) = Your Authenticity Assessment Score.

Note: Your scores for (A + B + C) and (X + Y + Z) MUST be the same number; otherwise you have a mathematical error. Your final score comes by adding these two numbers together.

B. Score Interpretation

There are two basic ways to look at scores. Most of us take tests and look for our 'score' and what the score means. Then we assess if we feel it is accurate or not. You now know your score and what follows is the chart from which to assess your score. But don't stop there. Be sure to read the interpretation to discover the deeper way to interpret your scores.

If you would like to learn more about any of the dimensions of the Authenticity Grid, you can visit http://TheInventories.com. There you will find a workbook for each of the nine dimensions. Each inventory contains exercises that guide you to gain more knowledge about yourself within that dimension. Some ask you to seek the opinion of others and some ask you to take an introspective look into yourself. Each enables you to broaden your perspective and identify ways to become more confident within that dimension. For example, if you want to increase your intuitive nature, the Intuition inventory will guide you through eight steps that will assist you to increase your alignment with your Inner Voice. As you strengthen one or more of the dimensions, you will find yourself becoming more confident, altering your perspective and basically gaining a deeper level of self-knowledge. It's like taking a journey inside of yourself and emerging with a new and expanded view of your possibilities. Enjoy!

165 – 180 ♥ Authentically Authentic

Congratulations! You know yourself and have taken time to integrate positive practices into your life. What you give to people is a true representation of who you are, and you are probably engaged in a career that is rewarding and satisfying. Being authentic is easy for you because you are clear about who you are, your purpose and you have developed an authentic life.

150 – 164 ♥ Appreciably Authentic

You are on your way to being authentically authentic. You have integrated many positive practices into your life and are working on improving more aspects of your life. People appreciate your honest sharing and look for more from you. As you continue to express your Inner and Outer Voices you will enhance your authenticity. Keep up the good work!

135 – 149 ♥ Approaching Authenticity

With a little effort, you will be authentically authentic. Identify the areas where your scores are lowest and focus on integrating the concepts into your life. Tweak your thinking and modify your habits to attain greater authenticity.

120 – 134 ♥ Almost Authentic

You are aware that you have not attained your highest level of authenticity, yet you are a little confused about how to attain it. Perhaps you feel like you are going in circles in spite of your efforts. Take some time and focus on the areas where your scores are lowest. Successfully work on one area at a time and your life will become more synergetic; you will gain energy and authenticity.

105 – 119 ♥ A Little Authentic

Take time and get to know yourself on a deeper level. In order to adequately connect with people, you need to achieve a level of authenticity that gives you the freedom to be yourself. People who have found a higher level of authenticity are generally more successful in life, connecting with people, finding their purpose and living a more rewarding and satisfying life.

Under 105 ♥ A Need to Be Authentic

Authenticity stems from self-knowledge and self-expression. Without each of these, it is difficult to find your purpose and live a rewarding and satisfying life. Being authentic means expressing your true self. First, find yourself. You will benefit from the programs we offer to strengthen your authentic voice. Contact us at 323-734-7144 or Coaching@NormaHollis.com.

In addition to the above, go a little deeper by assessing the following:

Step #1: Look at your A, B and C scores. Which are higher and which are lower? Your highest score is generally your 'default' style, your 'come from,' how you show up. Most people are either more Inner Voice-, Outer Voice- or Expressive Voice-oriented. Inner Voice people rely a lot on Intuition to make decisions and communicate with others. Outer Voice-dominant people generally understand the ways of the world and flow within it. Expressive Voice people are generally happily expressing themselves but sometimes unclear of how to align their Inner and Outer Voices.

Step #2: Look at your X, Y and Z scores. Which are higher and which are lower? Most people benefit from having someone on their team who has the opposite energy as they do. For example, a leader whose horizontal score is THINK may be superb at planning and strategizing projects and activities. However, such a leader needs to have team members who are strong in the DO energy because these are the people who will turn the ideas into reality.

Step #3: Identify the dimension where you had the lowest score. Decide on one thing to tweak in that one dimension. Once this tweak has been integrated in your life, find something else to tweak. Just tweak one thing at a time and reassess in six months to see how you, your life and your team have changed.

Step #4: If you have the same scores in any of the previous instructions, you decide which of them is most critical and proceed accordingly.

There was a time when all leaders strived to be perfect, to be all things to all people. Now we know this is not needed and not possible to achieve. The authentic leader is aware of the aspects of the Authenticity Grid where they have weakness. They are not afraid to admit to their weakness and they actively seek to hire people who have the strengths that the authentic leader does not.

Explore the Inner, Outer and Expressive Voices of your team members and align them with the inner, outer and expressive tasks that must be accomplished.

When you are clear on your Inner Voice, in command of your Outer Voice and fully expressing your Expressive Voice, you are a happy individual who is living with great authenticity.

If you want to go deeper with your understanding call 323-734-7144 or email Coaching@NormaHollis.com and let's discuss the ways we can support you as you develop your authentic leadership skills.

Chapter 7

The Importance of Alignment

A. Authentic Leaders Align Their Personal Mission with the Mission of the Company

The qualities of authentic leaders work best when the leader is aligned with the mission of the organization. If that alignment is absent, these qualities lose their strength in the workplace.

We each have personal goals that drive our activities on a day-to-day basis. Some of us have a purpose or mission. These are not generally shared in the work environment although they drive our thoughts, communications and behaviors, even when we are at work. Sometimes we are clearly aware of our personal goals, purpose or mission and sometimes we only know that they exist but have not identified them.

Likewise, all companies have a mission statement. The mission statement articulates what the company is all about, what it is seeking to achieve. Generally, the greater the clarity of the mission statement, the easier employees can understand and embrace it.

The most authentic leaders work in companies where the leader's personal mission is aligned with the mission of the company. When this happens, the leader finds the work more meaningful and fulfilling; it's easier to be committed, loyal, engaged and authentic.

Research reveals that 70% of the US workforce is not engaged at work. Perhaps this is because work is often the robotic repetition of certain tasks that have no alignment with the individual's goals in life other than the ability to earn a living. For many people, that's not enough.

When the company mission and employee mission are aligned, the employee has a greater investment in the company and the work they are doing. And when the employee also has the opportunity to use their natural gifts and talents in their day-to-day work, there is greater opportunity for engagement and loyalty.

The Bottom Line

Authentic leaders who are ready to inspire their teams get to know the natural gifts and talents of team members and help them integrate their gifts and talents into the work environment. When they have a joyful approach to the job, express their personality in authentic ways and keep themselves healthy, they will no doubt build the rapport and engagement that is needed to create empowering experiences that transform organizations.

With this information, authentic leaders have the tools to balance the energy of the approaching Empowerment Age with the structure required for societal growth. As a result, you can produce transformative organizations where employees thrive.

ORGANIZATIONAL CASE STUDIES

In Chapters 8, 9 and 10 you will read case studies from the perspective of three individuals. Each is a student of authenticity and has used the Authentic Voice System in various professional ways. Chapters 8 and 9 are from health care industry professionals, and Chapter 10 is from a former Vice President of Human Resources at a major retailer.

Entering the conversation on authentic leadership are two health care professionals. Peggy Muhammad has been a registered nurse for 40 years. She has taught the Authentic Voice principles to multiple audiences of nurse leaders. Dr. Dexter Russell applies the concepts of authenticity to the alternative health care industry. With the current medical system driven by chemical-based solutions and the multitude of debates on how health care is paid for, both agree that this is one industry that could benefit from a transformation to authentic leadership.

Chapter 8

Authenticity for Health Care Leaders

Peggy Muhammad, BSN, RN

A Registered Nurse's Perspective

Over the course of more than four decades as a nurse, I have come to learn how important authenticity is in the nursing environment. I decided to explore specifically how I could use authenticity to improve the care of patients and communities, promote healthy lifestyles, commit more to my value system, include diversity, be a better advocate and establish more harmony between body, mind and spirit within myself and my patients.

My research led me to understand what it meant to be authentic. I learned that being authentic meant being a skilled communicator, practicing with heart, establishing nurturing relationships, practicing self-discipline, being true to myself and my values and acting accordingly. While all of these recommendations are important to the nursing environment, they don't speak to 'how' to create authenticity in the work environment.

That's when I found the Authentic Voice System, a paradigm for authenticity that promotes more rewarding relationships between employees and employer, customers and business organizations, and individuals and community. I believe that the study and mindful practice of authenticity can transform the individual and advance the profession.

I have been trained on the use of the Authenticity Grid and have shared the information with nurses within the San Antonio Military Medical Center (SAMMC). As a result, I believe that all nurses, whether clinical or leader, novice or veteran, can learn to create environments of authenticity if they employ the Authentic Voice System's multidimensional approach to achieving alignment with one's nature, spirit and character. They need only develop an awareness of self that includes listening to, trusting in and following the energy produced by their Inner Voice.

My own experience with my Inner Voice and authenticity was transformative. When it came to critical thinking I was more concerned with evidence-based information and shoved Intuition to the back of my mind. At one point in my career I was confronted with having to administer a high dose of a medication after a cardiac procedure. The one-time order for that particular medication was reasonable for the cardiac procedure. The nurse who gave me the report never mentioned that she had already given the medication, so when I saw the order, there was no reason for me to question it.

When I attempted to enter the medication room to obtain the medication, I experienced a severe abdominal upset. It was so severe that I had to sit down until it went away. I tried to enter the medication room two more times and each time I got the same result. I finally accepted the message that my Intuition was sending. I called the nurse who gave me the report to determine if she had already given the medication and her answer was in the affirmative. She failed to check the 'given' icon so that the order would go away. I sincerely believe that listening to and following through with the instructions from my Intuition saved a patient and two nurses from the fallout surrounding a horrible medication error.

As I continued exploring authenticity in my work as a nurse I learned that nurses who create authentic environments practice with Integrity and are aligned with their personal or professional values. They are inspired to overcome challenges and to act on behalf of their patients and colleagues in spite of difficulty or opposition. They are purposeful and passionate about what they do. These are examples of their Outer Voice. These nurses are your colleagues who demonstrate physical, emotional and spiritual wellness. Nurses who create authentic environments have strong professional and personal networks that they utilize on behalf of their patients, colleagues and themselves. They understand that Net Wealth is not just financial, but the A-Z accumulation of accomplishments, blessings, grace, health, intelligence, opportunities, wisdom and zeal.

These nurses also have an Expressive Voice that is the result of honoring and using their God-given gifts and talents. They are generally likeable people who make excellent first impressions and have a calming effect on the people around them. Their lifestyles are passionate expressions of their attitudes, tastes and values expressed through their day-to-day habits.

Nurses who are aligned with their nature, spirit and character are well on the way to establishing healthy work environments. These are the nurses who can best create environments that are patient-centered, nurse-friendly, respectful, collegial, culturally relevant, creative, purposeful, as well as physically and emotionally safe where nurses, other health professionals and the community work together.

Authenticity indeed has a place in the nursing environment. It is an efficient and necessary component that will make the research come alive. As nurses we have a responsibility to step into a level of authenticity that enables us to impact our environments of care. We become role models for the health profession when we accept the invitation to be authentic.

Chapter 9

An Alternative Health Care Practitioner's Perspective on Authentic Leadership

Dexter S. Russell, DN

The overriding purpose of this chapter is to lend a voice to alternative medicine and its role in the delivery of effective health care in America. By all accounts we have a health system in crisis that continues to operate using obsolete management models that are not sustainable. To avert the potential collapse of the system, we need leaders who are game changers and have the ability to implement transformational ideas. Another leadership quality important for success is the ability to affect human motivation and performance while also managing huge capital resources and navigating bureaucratic obstacles.

Authenticity in leadership is an emerging model that is gaining acceptance in many industries across the country. Authentic leaders are not only competent in their respective fields, they also possess a social morality that places people over profit, and an understanding of the essential nature of life. While the political debate continues in Washington, DC regarding which health care system is right for the country, it is important to note that data from the Centers for Medicare and Medicaid Services (CMS) project suggests that by 2025 health care spending will represent nearly 20% of the GDP, up from the current 18%. It is my contention that the increasing acceptance of alternative medicine by the mainstream health care system will contribute to cost savings over the long run. Many alternative therapies work by helping the body to heal itself, require less invasive procedures and are generally less expensive.

Increasingly, a growing number of people are turning to alternative methods to address their health care needs. Witness the increased acceptance of traditional Chinese medicine and acupuncture, homeopathy, manual therapies such as osteopathy, chiropractic, naprapathy and massage as well as herbal and nutritional supplements combined with special diets. Patients are voicing their appreciation for health care practitioners who can combine aspects of the mind-body-spirit connection and treat them as a whole being. This holistic approach is gaining in popularity and empowers patients to take more responsibility for their health and well-being. Although conventional medicine earns high marks for handling medical emergencies, trauma, and complicated invasive procedures, it has been less than stellar in treating chronic illnesses. Chronic conditions are the leading cause of doctor's office visits and hospitalization.

A more recent phenomenon taking place in the health care marketplace is the increasing number of prominent medical facilities that have established integrative medical departments as part of the clinical setting. Proven effective alternative therapies, referred to as Complementary and Alternative Medicine (CAM), are now part of the clinical environment. To that end several medical schools have added courses in alternative and natural medicine as part of their curriculum. This level of authenticity should be applauded. Doctors will be facing consumers of health care who are results-oriented and looking for answers that they believe have not been fully addressed by conventional medicine.

I lay out in the following pages my journey as an alternative health practitioner and the role the authenticity paradigm has played in my personal transformation and that of my practice. First, I will share how I became involved in the authenticity community and the influence this has had on my outlook. Second, I will show how my clinical practice evolved into a holistic wellness entity following the principles of authenticity. Finally, I will present a case study of a patient who directly benefited after being introduced to the concept of authentic health and wellness intervention.

Background

I am a doctor of naprapathic medicine with studies in nutrition, dietetics, craniosacral therapy and polarity therapy. I have been granted membership in the Sacred Medical Order of the Knights of Hope, a global organization of medical practitioners delivering health screenings and care to underserved communities in different parts of the world. The Knights of Hope are carrying on the lineage of ecclesiastical and monastic medicine – the forerunner to naturopathic medicine. Ecclesiastical medicine encompasses treatment of illness based on natural laws governing the human body. It aims to restore and maintain health as well as to prevent and treat physical, mental and spiritual illness.

Naprapathic medicine is uniquely American in its origin. Founded in 1903 by Dr. Oakley Smith, an Iowa physician, it shares a connection to the manual healing arts of osteopathy and chiropractic medicine.

In 2010 I was at a crossroads in my career as a naprapath. I had been in practice for ten years and while I enjoyed working with patients in a clinical setting I was feeling unfulfilled and questioned whether I was living up to my full potential. I spent hours searching for answers in self-help books and motivational materials. However, the answer continued to elude me. I consulted a mentor who suggested that I give community lectures on alternative health and healing.

The strategy was for me to develop my speaking skills or even become a wellness coach. Following a brief period of consideration, I began to search for a public speaking training program. My search led me to an organization run by Norma Hollis, an accomplished public speaker, author and coach in Los Angeles. This discovery was a pivotal moment for me. She operated a speakers' bureau and had trained many prominent individuals in the business of public speaking. Additionally, she had coached and mentored many prominent people to success in their professional careers.

After reading Norma's book *Ten Steps to Authenticity*, I was convinced I had found the tutor I had been searching for. Authenticity as a tool for personal development was new to me and the promise that this knowledge could help create a rewarding and satisfying life was quite appealing. It wasn't long before I enrolled in the training to become an Authenticity Ambassador.

Personal Transformation

In my determination to move forward with my professional and personal life as an Authenticity Ambassador, I decided to implement the Authentic Voice System (AVS) developed by Norma after resuming my clinical practice. Knowing that it takes time to integrate new information I resisted the temptation of trying to use all I had learned and to take a more deliberate approach to how I would use this knowledge. This is how I used the Authentic Voice System to guide me on my path.

Inner Voice

Intuition is a key component of the Inner Voice that is constantly speaking to us day in and day out. The ability to listen to that Inner Voice and capture what is being said requires focus and attention. I had practiced meditation at various times in my life but was not consistent. To tap into my Intuition, I scheduled time in a quiet place free from external distractions. Once comfortably seated, I took a few deep breaths and closed my eyes as I slowly exhaled. Next, I observed my thoughts. At first this was not easy to do. Finding stillness in my mind was a huge challenge due to the incessant chatter inside my head. When thoughts of abandoning my efforts to still the mind would come up I resisted and remained seated. Then a peculiar thing would happen.

After a few minutes my thoughts and breathing would naturally start to slow down, and I discovered that by slowing my breath and visualizing a gently flowing stream, I became calmer. My thoughts would then become even slower. A state of deep relaxation would come over me as I watched each thought float by. Occasionally one of the thoughts would grab my attention and I allowed it to dominate my sense of awareness. Sometimes the thought I was focusing on came with a feeling attached to it and I would write key words or phrases on a notepad for later interpretation.

The more I sat in silence the better I became at catching insights and ideas that had never before appeared on a conscious level. On one occasion a memory about a passion fruit vine running on a chain-link fence at a home where I had lived 20 years earlier presented itself. I jotted down the word *passion* on my notepad as a reminder to look more closely at what that meant. Several hours later when I picked up the notepad a clear thought popped into my mind, saying, "Follow your passion," which repeated itself like a mantra. I began a list of things I felt passionate about and discovered that wellness and spirituality were at the top of the list.

Around this time, I was not very physically active due to a nagging knee injury that was healing slowly. Jogging had been my preferred form of exercise but I avoided it, so I wouldn't delay my recovery. I found a personal trainer who introduced me to ELDOA, a form of stretching and strengthening exercise techniques developed by a French osteopath, Guy Voyer, and I fell in love with working out again. As my physical training became more intense and my level of fitness improved, my energy level went way up, as did the number of hours I was spending at work giving treatments. It didn't take long for me to realize that I needed to balance my activities with more rest and relaxation.

I began noticing signs of burnout approaching and returned to the Authentic Voice System for guidance. There I was reminded that you cannot live a fully authentic life in a body that is not responding as it should. My attention now shifted to my Outer Voice and its principle surrounding wellness and balance, namely Net Wellness.

Outer Voice

There are some things that many health care practitioners would not readily admit. One is that we don't always practice what we preach. Having knowledge about the human body and what's required to maintain it is not enough. Motivation and discipline are two imperative pieces of the wellness puzzle, and if those are missing, neglect often occurs.

I make it a point to discuss with my patients the importance of taking care of the whole being. Staying in my authenticity meant that I had to become healthy and be a role model. It was at this point when I started sharing. I taught my patients tips for stretching their backs while they were at work. They were encouraged to incorporate more organic foods into their diet, get sufficient sleep, increase hydration and do some form of movement exercise. I provided the latest effective information on weight management and techniques on how to control stress. I was building a wellness practice with an emphasis on the whole person.

I share an office with other practitioners, who told me that they noticed the increase in the number of patients coming to see me for care. They were curious as to what had changed that was attracting these people.

My answer was that by following my passion for health and healing I was led to my true purpose for being on Earth. That brought me into alignment with my natural gift and talent as a visionary healer. Becoming aligned influenced my work, which accounted for the positive treatment results my patients were experiencing. This revelation prompted me to consult the Authentic Voice System, as I periodically do, and it became evident to me that I was operating in my Expressive Voice mode under the Legacy dimension. Patients who are satisfied with the care they are receiving generally refer family and friends.

Expressive Voice

The best explanation I could offer my colleagues was that I was using my natural gifts and talent in what I did and thus the patients were benefiting from my authenticity. I now feel a sense of gratitude knowing that I am fulfilling my purpose in this life.

Case Study – *T, a 56-year-old woman, came to my office for treatment of chronic upper back pain. With her regular monthly treatments, she experienced a recurring pattern of relief for a period of time, then stiffness in the spine and upper musculature, resulting in more pain. Over the years I'd been treating T, it became apparent that her work environment had been partly responsible for her health condition. As part of her treatment protocol I emphasized the importance of diet and exercise along with proper sleep hygiene. T followed my advice and showed signs of improved health. However, due to lack of consistency and discipline T would revert to old patterns that did not support a healthy Lifestyle.*

I came to realize that I needed a system to guide her in staying with her intention of experiencing vibrant health on a continuous basis. I introduced her to the Authentic Voice System and began to focus on the principles of Net Wellness and Lifestyle. As T's awareness grew, the topic of authenticity began to take on a new meaning for her wellness and well-being. T now had a structured system of self-accountability and realized how much power she had over her health and Lifestyle behavior. T became more interested in the other AVS principles and began to embrace the Inner Voice of Intuition and Inspiration. As T's confidence grew so did her enthusiasm, and on one of her office visits she stated that her pain episodes were fewer and further apart. In addition, she reported sleeping better, having more energy and noticing less stress at work.

When I asked her what she attributed her improved outlook to, she said without hesitation, "I have more control over the events in my life because I have a structured system that guides my thoughts and actions." T now comes to see me every six to eight weeks because she is pain free. Her case is an example of the transformative results that can occur when an authentic way of life is adopted and in alignment with what we most care about.

Conclusion

The challenges facing our health care system are complex and require creative leadership to bring about changes needed for the 21st century. Alternative medicine modalities with a proven track record of effectiveness in treating illness and disease stand ready to be part of the solution. One tool that has been proven to facilitate change on the personal and institutional level is the Authentic Voice System created by Norma Hollis.

Leaders charged with delivering health care in the 21st century will need to become agents for change. Through personal and organizational transformations brought about by the increased self-awareness of health care leaders, one can expect to see a new paradigm guided by intuitive knowledge that is compassionately expressed.

Chapter 10

Authentic Leadership for Employee Retention

Betty Kimbrough, BS

Former Vice President of Human Resources for Target Stores

HR executives all over the world will tell you that keeping good people is critical to the success of any organization. Finding those people falls squarely in the HR purview. However, keeping them is a total team effort. It is a leadership effort. And it requires authentic leadership.

Thus far, we have focused on what it takes to be an authentic leader. It can be taught, learned and developed at the individual level. But more importantly, it can and must be cultivated at the organizational level to have the desired impact on retention.

Over the years we have seen annual increases get smaller, so millennials and boomers alike have found it more lucrative to change jobs, or change companies, to experience meaningful salary growth. And then there are benefits. With the rising cost of healthcare, childcare and the ever-elusive retirement age, the need for medical coverage, flexible spending accounts and retirement benefits is more important than ever.

Why Do Employees Leave?

When you ask employees why they left their last company, most often they will tell you it was for a better job, more money or more opportunity. Yet if you dig beneath the surface, and ask the right questions, you'll start to get the real reasons. They left because they didn't feel compelled to stay. They didn't feel connected to the organization. They didn't feel connected to their supervisor or their co-workers. They didn't believe they mattered enough, or what was important to them didn't matter enough, to anyone to stay. Employee retention goes beyond dollars and cents. Emotions are often at the heart of the matter.

It has been said many times that "Employees don't leave companies. They leave bosses." The fact is, they leave both. They may tell you on the way out the door that they left for a better job or more money. But what they are really saying is they left in search of the connection they didn't have at your organization. People leave for a variety of reasons. But they will stay if they feel connected.

So, what is this missing connection? The boss who 'gets' them? The recognition of the contribution they make? The opportunity to learn something new? The mission of the company? The values of the organization? The comradery of the team they work with? The answer is all of the above. What is missing is engagement. How do you get it? Authentic leadership.

Back in the day, when I was an HR Director for Target Stores' distribution centers, I asked my boss to make me bonus eligible. The HR Directors in the Stores part of our company were bonus eligible. My business partners, the GMs of those distribution centers were bonus eligible. In fact, all director-level positions in the field were eligible to receive a bonus for their performance and contribution to company profitability. That is, all except me. When she told me that I wouldn't get a bonus, that it just wasn't possible, I became disillusioned. I had been at Target for nine years. Although I had steadily moved up in the organization, I didn't feel that my contribution was valued as much as others at the same level, doing the same type of work as I was.

So, when another organization came knocking on my door, I answered. They offered me an opportunity to be the head of HR, reporting to the CEO, with more money and bonus eligibility. I accepted.

On the eve of what was to be my last day at Target, at my going-away party, my boss' boss, who was the Senior Vice President of Human Resources and my mentor, asked me why I was really leaving. I told him more responsibility, more money, and a VP title. He said, "You can have all of that at Target and you know it. So why are you really leaving?" I told him that I felt disrespected and undervalued. I had gone to my boss and she basically said forget it. It's not going to happen. I'm certain she didn't say it that way, but that's the way I heard it. I didn't feel like anyone cared if I stayed or left. So, when another company came along and made me feel like I really did deserve the respect and compensation I was looking for, I went for it.

My mentor proceeded to tell me what he saw as my career path and how my experiences to date were preparing me for that. Then he wrote a counter offer on a paper napkin and asked me to reconsider. If I would give the company another chance, he would see me in the morning. That night I decided to stay. It was much more than the numbers on the napkin that brought me to that decision. It was the fact that he cared enough to ask and then to make me feel like a valued part of the team.

That next morning, I announced to the HR team that I was staying. The CEO of Target and the CEO of the Dayton Hudson Corporation, our parent company, each came to my office to shake my hand and thank me for staying. That meant so much to me! I went on to stay another 13 years at Target.

I didn't know what to call it back then, but I knew there was a lesson there. Today I call it *authentic leadership.*

Engagement and Well-Being

While it is true that money is important to just about everyone, it will only go so far because no matter how much you pay, there is always more money to be had. Once you meet the basic needs, we begin to look for challenges, career paths, learning opportunities, community, appreciation and people who care.

Therefore, it is incumbent upon the authentic leader to be tuned in to his or her team members to understand what they need and attempt to help them meet those needs within the organization. This is what we call tapping into Intuition, listening to and understanding the ideas and needs of the team, keeping your finger on the pulse of the team. Taking it a step further, creating an environment that enhances their overall well-being, will lead to inspired action, increased productivity and employee engagement. It will also help you see and impact those on the team that are not engaged.

The best definition I have seen for employee engagement is "the emotional commitment the employee has to the organization and its goals." That can only be there if the employee understands what the organization is about and feels inspired to be a part of it.

The Gallup organization has done a great deal of research in the areas of employee engagement and well-being, both of which they concluded are key to employee retention (Sorenson 2013). Minimally, offering a competitive salary and benefit program (financial well-being) and providing the necessary tools and workspace to do the job (physical well-being) are a start. But to impact engagement and retention, you also have to tap into the social, community and purpose aspects of employee well-being. You have to tap into those items that involve emotions in order to create that feeling of connection.

Legacy

Let's take purpose, for example. To cultivate authentic leadership in your organization, it is imperative to not only understand what each team member brings to the table, but to help them see how they contribute to the mission of the organization.

Senior leadership must first answer the questions:

- What do we do best?
- What is our competitive advantage?
- How do we contribute to the community we live and work in?

This is Legacy at the organization level. The senior leadership team must have a strong understanding of the organization's Legacy and be able to articulate that to the rest of the team. This not only provides clarity for the entire team, but also generates a feeling of pride for each individual to see their employer 'winning' and contributing in the communities they are a part of.

From there, each leader must understand what they do best:

- What are my natural gifts and talents?
- How can I use them to contribute to the mission of the organization?
- How does this fit with the rest of the team?

There is a much greater chance of anyone being inspired to do the work and be engaged within the organization if they get to do what they know and love to do. And there is a greater chance of organizational success if the leadership team understands how they can support each other using the natural gifts and talents of each leader.

I once worked with a leadership team made up of what appeared to be basically the same profile. The organization had decided what 'type' of leader was the most successful and selected accordingly. Internal candidates for promotion to these positions learned what was rewarded and behaved that way, even when it went against their nature. The result was a stressful environment for those leaders, as they had to suppress their natural selves, and also for the team members who were often at the receiving end of stress-induced behavior. When we started problem-solving with the leadership team, we determined that they were missing some key abilities among them. For example, all knew how to be strong operators. Few knew how to develop talent. Also, when we worked with individual leaders, we found that in some instances, they were hesitant to utilize some of their natural gifts and talents for fear of being viewed as weak. They needed to 'unlearn' some behaviors and to be reinforced for others. When the opportunity presented itself, we ended up adding members to the team who had the missing skillsets. We did so, telling them up front that they may feel some resistance initially from peers who were not accustomed to using certain skills. We needed them to model the behaviors/skill set and let others see them being reinforced for them. We were seeding the team with authentic leaders so as to change the culture of the organization.

Assessing and sharing natural gifts and talents as a team allows leaders to see what they are missing and identify ways to supplement and/or develop the leadership team. But more importantly, it also allows the team to learn something about each other that they may not have known, making it easier to help each other succeed. If you know what gifts they bring to the table, you can utilize them to the benefit of the individual and the organization.

This is Legacy, one aspect of authentic leadership that demonstrates what kind of organization yours has become, what kind of leaders yours have become and what kind of workforce yours has become. It demonstrates the culture your employees come to work in and will obviously have a profound effect on what they experience on a day-to-day basis. Impact your organization's Legacy and you will impact employee engagement. Impact engagement and you will impact retention.

Culture

What kind of culture do you have? What is your employee experience? Whenever I interview a leader, I ask them to tell me about the culture of their current organization. I listen for insight and nuances and then ask them to compare and contrast that to what they know about the culture of the organization they want to join. It's a good way to get a read from an outside source. What do people say about your organization's culture? Who do they say you are versus who you say you are? You also need to know what your employees have to say about the culture. Who do they say you are and how does that compare?

When I joined Target Stores, the company had a reputation of being 'lean and mean.' I knew this going in and had decided I would probably only stay about five years at the most because the culture was one of using people up, burning them out and moving on. Turnover was high at all levels. I joined the company anyway because it had a strong commitment to community service and the HR department was well respected in the industry for level of talent and having a 'seat at the table.' I was willing to tolerate this type of culture in order to get the experience of working with and learning from this HR team.

Seven years into my tenure there, the HR team made a conscious effort to change the culture from 'lean and mean' to 'fast, fun and friendly.' It did not happen overnight and was a massive undertaking. It required getting leadership to understand the cultural shift and know how to model it. It also required convincing our team members that we meant for 'fast, fun and friendly' to apply to our interactions with them as well as our interactions with our guests. The culture did start to shift, and retention improved at all levels. There was an air of excitement, as you would expect when you have something new to rally everyone around – especially in this case, because it was all about how we treated our guests and each other.

The shift in culture impacted retention, individual performance and company performance. When it started to break down, and it did break down, it was because the leadership team didn't walk the talk. We were still a sales-driven organization and for some leaders, it was way too easy to lose sight of the team members.

Authentic leadership calls for us to keep our organizational values in mind as we run our day-to-day operations. If we want to keep good people, this has to be explicitly stated as part of the organization's values.

Habits and Rewards

We all know that if we want to make meaningful changes in our lives, it requires a change of mindset and habit. We have to change the way we think and what we do, how we spend our time. The same holds true for an organization and its culture. How your leaders spend their time, what they do, reflects what you believe is important. Intentions are only the beginning. You have to put practices/habits in place to back them up. What the organization rewards will impact results as well as the culture and ultimately retention.

If you have a 'leadership style' in an organization that gets rewarded, people tend to conform to that style in order to get ahead. The key, then, is to make sure you are rewarding the right things. In addition to the financial results or other measurements on the scorecard, you must cultivate authentic leadership by rewarding leaders who:

- Listen to and care about the well-being of their team
- Communicate openly and effectively
- Respect ideas of other team members
- Recognize and make the best use of the contributions, natural gifts and talents of team members
- Align their actions with the stated values and mission of the organization
- Effectively tie employee performance and contributions to the organization's purpose, mission and strength in the marketplace and/or community
- Model service in interactions with peers, team, and the community at large

Cultivating authentic leadership in your organization also requires cultivating good practices. It means teaching your leaders the habits that will bring about the desired results. One of the routines I practiced when I was in the field at Target, responsible for a single location, was to start each day on the floor at the distribution center talking to employees. When there was a shift change, again I walked the floor. I was out there, talking to people, asking questions about their work, their frustrations, their victories and understanding the flow of their work. I wasn't an unknown to them. They saw me every day. If there was something they wanted me to know, they would seek me out. If there was something I wanted to know about, they were eager to tell me. What makes this practice effective is the genuine caring a leader displays toward the team.

When I became responsible for multiple locations across the country, I spent three to four days per week visiting store and distribution center locations, with the same intention: connecting with people, understanding their issues and looking for ways to make their work lives better. The better their work lives, the better the organization's chances were of accomplishing the shared mission. Having senior leadership do these types of visits gives the opportunity for local leadership to understand what authentic leadership looks like, building trust, connecting, understanding what employees need to be successful and getting it for them, recognizing strengths and contributions that employees bring to the table, identifying and developing future leaders, role modeling, and so on. These visits cannot be punitive or abusive in any way. For just as the positive behaviors will be modeled, so will the negative. The key to boosting employee engagement and retention is creating a positive employee experience.

Creating a Positive Employee Experience

Take a close look. What is the employee experience in your organization? What do you see when you go to work? Are people collaborating? Are your employees struggling to get the resources they need to do their work? Do you see creativity? Do people appear genuinely caring and friendly toward one another? Are they frustrated with a lack of communication? Is there a pervasive sense of being unappreciated? Do people love to come to work every day? Is the competition healthy or unhealthy? Are people frustrated with all of the rules, policies and procedures? Are all of the procedures you have in place really necessary? Do you have to control everything so tightly? Can you allow some flexibility, some room for an employee to do it their way? These are all aspects of organizational culture that shape your employee experience. If you want to keep good people, you have to keep the environment, where they may spend eight to 12 hours per day, a positive one.

What's a Leader to Do?!

One way that the authentic leader can enhance or ensure employee engagement is to hold team members accountable for poor performance. Authentic leaders manage performance. They determine when additional training is called for or when an employee is simply misplaced. The important thing to remember is the other team members are paying attention to whether, and how, the leader handles the problem performer. It goes without saying that the organization and each of its employees has to perform. If you don't get results, you won't be a viable organization for long. Just as leaders want employees to perform, so do the other members of the team. They want and expect each member to do their part and pull their weight. However, when it becomes clear that the employee isn't capable of doing so, the authentic leader will handle it respectfully and in a timely manner.

Another common practice of authentic leaders is to seek feedback. They look for feedback on themselves, on their work and on their team. They look for feedback from their team, from their bosses, from their peers and from their customers. They are in a mode of continuous learning. They never assume they have all the answers and have a genuine curiosity, a sincere interest, in knowing more.

Authentic leaders continuously communicate the organization's values, vision and mission. They do so to constantly remind and reinforce what is important. They work alongside employees to see what they see and experience what they experience. This helps them identify any obstacles that need to be removed and validates their beliefs about what is really happening.

Transforming the Organization

To create, cultivate and sustain authentic leadership in an organization it is important to understand where you are today and where you want to be. Then make the commitment to get there. This is not an insignificant thing and requires buy-in at all levels of leadership. However, once you have set the intention and get the necessary buy-in, you can begin to create an authentic employer brand and develop a plan that will begin to transform the organization's culture. Who do you want to be as an employer?

You can begin to create and communicate a compelling vision of your values and mission as an organization.

You can begin to hire the right people. People whose goals, values and skills are in step with the organization is a start. Hiring leaders who have a high degree of emotional intelligence, however, provides a great foundation for developing authentic leaders and cultivating an authentic organization.

You can begin to assess, develop and build on the strengths of each member of the team, recognizing the contribution each one makes to the mission of the organization.

You can begin to foster an environment where people can learn and grow. Development and growth opportunities don't always have to mean promotions.

You can begin to manage performance in an inspiring manner, treating employees with dignity and respect. Let people know where they stand through ongoing coaching conversations, not just at review time. Give them the means to measure their own performance on a regular basis. Authentic leaders communicate and coach.

You can begin to reinforce and reward the behaviors that contribute to the culture of authenticity.

Cultivating Authentic Leadership

I gave a talk to a group of students and educators at St. Cloud State University. My message to them was about knowing the difference between learning how to act versus learning how to be. We obviously need to know how to act. We start learning that from a very young age. Have you ever heard a parent of an 'out of control' toddler say, "You better act like you have some sense!" Or, they might say, "We don't act like that in public." We quickly learn that we are to act certain ways in certain circumstances. The same is true in organizations. When you join an organization, you get the lay of the land, and you learn what behavior is appropriate and what is not. You learn how to act.

But, who teaches us how to 'be'? When you strip away all of the false packaging and become aware of who you are and what makes you tick, you will begin to know how to 'be.' We cannot be something we're not, although it's human nature to try again and again. We all want to fit in. We try on different packaging until we find something that feels right. We try connecting with different people and organizations until we find what feels right. Sometimes we try to stick it out when it doesn't feel right (relationships, careers, companies). However, when it doesn't feel right, it probably isn't. We have to show our leaders how to 'be.'

We have to teach them what authentic leadership is and raise the awareness level of their own authenticity. We have to teach them that, day in and day out, it's:

- How you show up
- How you think
- How you communicate
- What you do
- What you tell yourself
- Who you surround yourself with
- How you treat yourself, your peers and your team members
- Servant leadership

The path to authentic leadership is through awareness and accountability. We have to teach them what authentic leadership can do for them, individually and collectively. We have to inspire them to continue developing their own authenticity and that of the organization. Then measure progress at the individual leader level and at the organization level. This is a prerequisite for success in creating a healthy organizational culture of high performance, synergy and engagement. Top talent needs a reason to stay with an organization. Being a part of an authentic leadership culture is just such a reason.

Enlightened organizations value authenticity in their leaders and in their culture. Being authentic as a leader only happens if the organization encourages it and if authenticity fits the organizational norms. This is why it is critical that new employees, as well as existing employees, understand who you are, what is important and what the culture of the organization is. Communicating this must be part of the selection process, the orientation process, and regular communications with your teams.

Authentic leadership matters because it can further the mission of the organization. It matters because it will bring out the best of each individual team member. It matters because when times get tough, the organization will be in the best position to ride it out. It matters because we are all here as individuals and organizations to make a unique contribution in service to others and authentic leadership shows us how we can best do that. It all comes down to an organization remaining focused and vigilant of its mission, culture, people and authenticity.

If you would like to go to the next step and apply the concepts to your organization, we would love to assist you. Authentic leadership is a competitive advantage for individual leaders and organizations alike. For you as an individual leader, we begin by raising your awareness of your own authenticity and where your strengths and vulnerabilities lie.

As an organization, we begin by assessing the authenticity strengths and vulnerabilities of your leadership team and the organization overall. We will then work with you to create a strategic plan to develop your team and create a culture of authenticity.

Call 323-734-7144 or email us at Coaching@NormaHollis.com and let's discuss the ways we can help you cultivate authentic leadership in your organization.

Conclusion

Authentic leadership is at the forefront of successful organizations in the 21st century. Baby boomers are demanding it, millennials are demanding it, and all employees in between and upcoming are demanding it. Successful organizations are no longer those that follow authoritative industrial age leadership. Instead, success comes when employees feel embraced, engaged, and respected. You can create this in your organization through authentic leaders.

Follow the blueprint offered in this book to give you, the leaders in your organization, and the organization as a whole the pathway to success through engagement. It is the wave of the future and a necessary step for organizations that want to be cutting edge and play an important role in building a culture of engagement among the employees and customers whom they serve.

Bibliography

Advisory.com. *CMS: US Health Care Spending to Reach Nearly 20% of GDP by 2025.* https://www.advisory.com/daily-briefing/2017/02/16/spending-growth

Carruthers, Tracey. *Life Under the Influence of Clear, Effective Thinking.* Long Beach, CA: Tracey Carruthers, 2008.

Gardner, Howard. *Multiple Intelligences: New Horizons in Theory and Practice.* New York: Basic Books, 2006.

George, Bill. "The Truth About Authentic Leaders." *Harvard Business School,* July 6, 2016, https://hbswk.hbs.edu/item/the-truth-about-authentic-leaders

George, Bill. "What Does Authentic Leadership Really Mean?" *HuffPost,* November 17, 2015, https://www.huffingtonpost.com/bill-george/what-does-authentic-leade_b_8581814.html

Gilmore, James H. & Pine, B. Joseph II. *What Consumers Really Want: Authenticity.* Boston, MA: Harvard Business Press, 2007.

Hollis, Norma. *Ten Steps to Authenticity: Creating a Rewarding and Satisfying Life.* Los Angeles, CA: Rhythm of the Drum, 2008.

Ibarra, Herminia. "The Authenticity Paradox." *Harvard Business Review,* January–February 2015, https://hbr.org/2015/01/the-authenticity-paradox

Keegan, Paul. "The 5 New Rules of Employee Engagement." *Inc. Magazine,* December 2014–January 2015, https://www.inc.com/magazine/201412/paul-keegan/the-new-rules-of-engagement.html

Kruse, Kevin. "What is Authentic Leadership?" *Forbes,* May 12, 2013, https://www.forbes.com/sites/kevinkruse/2013/05/12/what-is-authentic-leadership/#cdf938edef77

Kusch, Fred. "Managing the Heart and Soul of your Organization." *JFK Associates,* July 2, 2012, www.jfkassociates.com/2012/07/managing-the-heart-and-soul-of-your-organization-2/

Robbins, Anthony. *Awaken the Giant Within.* New York: Free Press, 1991.

Sorenson, Susan. "How Employee Engagement Drives Growth." *Gallup,* 2013. http://news.gallup.com/businessjournal/163130/employee-engagement-drives-growth.aspx, 2013

Tencer, Daniel. "85% of Jobs That Will Exist in 2030 haven't Been Invented Yet: Dell." *Huff Post,* July 14, 2017, http://www.huffingtonpost.ca/2017/07/14/85-of-jobs-that-will-exist-in-2030-haven-t-been-invented-yet-d_a_23030098/

Williams, Roy H. & Drew, Michael R. *Pendulum: How Past Generations Shape Our Present and Predict Our Future.* New York: Vanguard Press, 2012.

Winiarski, Pete & Levine, Terri. *The Innovators.* Melbourne, FL: Motivational Press, 2017.

Index